HOPE DISAPPEARING:
A POPULATION LEFT BEHIND

A Behind-the-Scenes Look at the Growing
Crisis of Homelessness in Our Nation

by Sherman Haggerty

IZZARD INK PUBLISHING
PO Box 522251
Salt Lake City, Utah 84152
www.izzardink.com

Library of Congress Cataloging-in-Publication Data

Names: Haggerty, Sherman, author.
Title: Hope disappearing : a population left behind : a behind-the-scenes
   look at the growing crisis of homelessness in our nation / by Sherman
   Haggerty.
Description: First edition. | Salt Lake City, Utah : Izzard Ink Publishing,
   [2021] | Includes index.
Identifiers: LCCN 2021028379 (print) | LCCN 2021028380 (ebook) |
   ISBN 9781642280692 (hardback) | ISBN 9781642280685 (paperback) |
   ISBN 9781642280678 (ebook)
Subjects: LCSH: Homelessness—United States. | Shelters for the homeless—United States. |
   Homeless persons—United States. | Homelessness—Government policy—United States. |
   Homeless persons—Services for—United States.
Classification: LCC HV4505 .H35 2021 (print) | LCC HV4505 (ebook) |
   DDC 362.5/0973—dc23
LC record available at https://lccn.loc.gov/2021028379
LC ebook record available at https://lccn.loc.gov/2021028380

Designed by Ashley Tucker
Cover Design by Andrea Ho
Cover Images: Philip Pilosian/Shutterstock.com

First Edition

Contact the author at info@izzardink.com

Hardback ISBN: 978-1-64228-069-2
Paperback ISBN: 978-1-64228-068-5
eBook ISBN: 978-1-64228-067-8

Contents

Dedications and Thanks

I am dedicating this book to the following three people who work for the local affiliate of Volunteers of America:

Leo McFarland, chief executive officer
Amani Sawires, chief operating officer
Christie Holderegger, chief development officer

Collectively, these three individuals have provided 100 years of service and leadership to the underserved, undervalued, and disenfranchised citizens of Northern California. They have led the effort to provide shelter, meals, and critical services to homeless singles, homeless families, and homeless veterans. They have also served those struggling with mental health, abused seniors, those struggling with addictions, and the many who were victims of life-changing events that no one could have predicted. I can say with absolute certainty that Volunteers of America has provided more services under their leadership, to more underserved people in the Sacramento region during the past 30 years than any other organization.

I also want to dedicate this work to a handful of remarkable, humble, selfless people whom I had the ability to observe or work directly with during my time at Mather Community Campus. I decided to choose a few to thank publicly in this publication, but there are dozens more; you know who you are and you should take great pride in knowing how important you were in helping to improve lives immeasurably. Also, enormous gratitude goes to the students who worked so hard to get through this program from 1996 to 2019 and have continued, years later, to make very significant contributions in our community. Some of their stories are a part of this work. Special thanks to:

Beth Maarten	Holly Sexton	Ellen O'Neal
John Reilly	Paula Moulten	Beth Valentine
Veronica Williams	Pat Fitzgerald	Marriane Friedrich
Terri Wheeler	Ruby Yang	Chris Mann
Elizabeth Garcia	Alan Knacke	Greg Williams
Jenna Winn	Connie Aaron	Mary Ann Wheeler*
Jimmy Smits	Erika Acosta	Sam Frank
Lynette Mabitun	Karen Christensen	Tom Crouse
Russ Miller	Haley Armstrong	Marlo Miller
Marcus Robinson	Kay Dowling	Carrie McCraken
Matt Printup	Sue Harlan	

*Including the entire staff from Next Move who stayed at Mather after the merger.

Introduction

This book is based on my and others' experiences working for Volunteers of America at a homeless transitional housing program in Northern California. These experiences represent the current changing landscape for the homeless population across the country and the future for them as citizens. (This work represents the views and opinion of the author and it is not intended to represent the opinions, views, or position of any private or public agency, business, or other individual.)

This book was written in an effort to raise concerns about the treatment of our homeless population; "hope disappearing" is not a cliché. It accurately reflected the future options for more than two hundred people over a 2-day period in the spring of 2017. These people were on a waiting list for comprehensive homeless services, a list that was eliminated by mandate. It was one isolated incident, in one community, but it signaled a change in the direction of homeless services across the country and the future for thousands of people. It was the indirect result of federal policy changes that had been in the works for over a decade. This book provides significant detail about how those changes impacted (and are still impacting) the structure of local homeless services. It also looks at the collateral damage to the homeless people and the communities where they live. If you do not care about the growing number of human beings who are homeless, the demise of their future potential, or its potential social impact, then this book is not for you.

By contrast, this book also shares the power of kindness and caring. It is getting a little difficult in our time to figure out whether caring is really an important part of the fabric of our country. We have all witnessed some radical behavior that we're told is the result of deep caring; however, the actions that have played out have more often hurt other people than helped them. Fortunately, I am an eternal optimist, especially about the majority of people in our community and the country. This book contains some remarkable true stories about the incredible impact kindness and caring made in the lives of individuals who had nowhere else to turn. Kindness is the tool we can use to open the damaged heart and help it to hope again. Caring can pave the path for hope to turn into opportunity.

I am critical in this book about the system that institutes sweeping policy changes from the federal level that ultimately impact the local community. I have strong opinions on why that system so often failed to produce the needed results. The culture that has developed inside of government offices at all levels does not promote or reward innovation or flexibility. The most influential decisions are being made by groups of people who are far removed from the problems they are supposed to address. That process leads to more problems than solutions. I hope to get you immersed in the complicated world of working through layers of government, when you have no authority, in the effort to serve the homeless.

Our local governments, being responsible for the administration of federal and state policies, have little power to alter those policies to fit regional needs. Attempts to work outside of federal policy guidelines can put the funding that is needed to do the work at risk. It is difficult to explain, but local social programs, dependent on federal funding, have been altered or defunded when they did not align with federal policy requirements. These decisions were not based on how effective those programs were at doing the work. The problem is reaching critical stages, with the effect of federal-level policies becoming evident in local homeless care. There are meetings recounted in this book (names not included) that highlight how difficult it is to fight that system, regardless of consequences. Our meetings were with local public officials. The substance and outcomes of those meetings are not intended to disparage any of them personally. *It is the system we continue to accept, which produces flawed policies that bind us, that needs to be restructured.*

It didn't occur to me to write a book about the homeless population and homeless care until all other avenues of expression and influence were eventually cut off. The seeds for this book were planted during a time when I felt desperate about witnessing the most progressive programming available to the homeless being dismantled for reasons I still do not understand. I am speaking specifically about the Mather Community Campus employment to housing program from 1996 through 2019. Providing the Mather example is necessary to showcase the homeless services that were in place prior to the impacts of federal policy changes. It will also show what obstacles people trying to exit homelessness can overcome with the right support and care. I believe the history of this program provides the perfect example of how federal policy impacted local homeless care, not just in our region but also across the nation. The after-effects of these actions are continuing to unfold in ways that should be concerning to all citizens.

It is important to repeat the statement here; that this work is not an attempt to discredit any individuals or their intentions. I am certain that the people and the agencies referenced in this book were doing the best they could with the resources that were available. Regardless, there were numerous attempts to speak with local government leaders, over a 2-year period, searching for alternative ways to keep that program open. In the end, a lot of time was spent in meetings and conversations that now seems wasted. It became obvious that the reasons we presented for keeping the employment to housing program alive were not going to substantiate the huge effort required to facilitate change. The decision to finally terminate the program came down to funding availability. Our local leaders decided that the Mather program model would not qualify for any new federal or state funds, and there were no funds in the local budget that could be reallocated. The Mather housing facilities are still in place and filled with homeless citizens. It is now being used as a shelter. I will lay out in detail the differences in the care provided before and after these changes. As I witnessed the closing of the employment program and the removal of critical services provided to clients, I came to this conclusion: We need to find a path to alter the current direction of homeless services to reinstate human decency and to move the use of taxpayers' funds in a more humane direction. This problem is not limited to Mather Campus.

What is depressing to this author about this particular example is that the incredible efforts and dedication of many people over a 24-year period, despite significant success, were left wanting. Thousands of homeless people were served through the employment program between 1997 and 2019. Many left homelessness for good. Compared to any other social service metric, based on the short- and the long-term impacts, both in outcomes and financial efficiency, the decision to abandon this model seems indefensible. The program won two national awards for excellence. Those awards happened after it was visited by representatives from the federal government in 2005 and 2007. It is a shame, but predictable, that there was no consideration to revisit the program again before disqualifying this model for future funding. I wrote to the then-acting director of the Department of Housing and Urban Development (HUD). The letter was a request for him to revisit and review the program that had been awarded for excellence before it was closed. There was no response.

There may be some who were involved locally in making the decision for this program to close who will claim that the model was outdated and did not fit the future of homeless services. The first part of that statement does not hold water. The program was being continually updated and improved based on services available, cost restrictions, and market trends for employment. The second half of the statement that refers to it not fitting the direction of future homeless services is accurate. That is another motivator for publishing this book, except that the word *services* should be removed in reference to these new homeless housing programs.

The current oversight of homeless care is not providing the tools to help this population find a road to self-sufficiency and the status of equality in the community that comes with achieving that goal. Do we even care about that? Do homeless lives matter? The current primary goal (as dictated by federal funding guidelines) for those in charge of managing the homeless is to get as many of them off of the street as possible, ready or not. The first six chapters of this book will give you a background on the policy issues that started the dehumanization of homeless services. In contrast, you should also get a good idea of what can happen when people really care about helping people who have been discarded as members of the community.

An equally important message in this book is that we should be deeply concerned for the future state of our communities, as the homeless population continues to grow in virtually every geographic segment. It is not just the problem of sheer population growth that is troubling; it is also the position that HUD has taken by abandoning responsibility to assist with treatment of drug and alcohol addiction and the related co-occurring mental health issues that plague the homeless. HUD also dropped funding support for most of the other critical services needed to provide many with the chance to become self-sufficient. Some of these services remain available in the community, but they have become scarce. They have been dropped as requirements from the new homeless program models that provide housing. Today there are very few publicly funded openings for alcohol and drug recovery or mental health treatment. These referral-based services require access to county funding, and the need for these services far outweighs their availability. Because the homeless housing models have no requirements for the client to access these services, and because they require travel to get to them, they have proven to be totally ineffective to meet the growing need.

A growing homeless population increases the difficulty of providing sanitation in public places. More human waste and used needles are left in public places where there are more homeless people. It is easy to blame the homeless for creating these issues, but it is really due to the lack of planning and availability. There are mounting problems with controlling drug-related crimes and the increased gang activity that comes with the use of drugs in the homeless population. There are future concerns to consider, as history has shown us that when the margin between the "haves" and the "have-nots" reaches an unbridgeable divide, it leads to serious social unrest.

This book is a story within a story. Think about the radio program the late great Paul Harvey used to host. He would often finish his show with a segment that he called "The Rest of the Story," which gave inside information on people or events that was not as readily known to the public as were the principals themselves. This book may actually be stories within stories within stories, so let's start with an explanation of how it has been put together. The foundation for presenting this work was developed over a 6-year period during which I had the honor to preside over an employment-based transitional housing program for homeless singles and families in

Northern California: Mather Community Campus. In 6 short years, this program went from the highest-rated program in our county (with the best outcomes and lowest recidivism rate of any homeless program it was measured against) to being totally dismantled and closed, a process that was tough on me personally as well as the rest of the staff.

The events that caused this to happen had nothing to do with the services, increased costs, internal problems with the program itself, or the wants and needs of the homeless population in the area. The demise started with a philosophical shift in the wind at the federal level that eventually choked off federal funding. Local officials eventually accepted the closing of this transitional housing and employment program. There was never more than minimal effort expended to seek new solutions. I asked many of these officials for their help with collaborating on new ideas. Their willingness to engage in meaningful discussion was lacking. In the end, they would claim it was the lack of new funding options. In fairness to those officials, it was an extremely complicated problem to overcome, and solutions were improbable under the existing circumstances. In time, these important issues should not remain impossible. We need the right minds and flexible attitudes to be able to overhaul the existing public spending initiatives.

It actually took 4 years to terminate the county contract for services that supported the work being done in the Mather employment program. It was a slow and difficult process and experience. The county contract was with the agency that was my employer at the time. Our agency had actually participated in the service work at Mather for over 20 years, including the six that I was the director. This book lays out in detail the objectives, communications, and working relationship between the county and the agency. It is a behind-the-scenes look at what being a government contractor entails, and the evolving process of aligning objectives and demands. There are also details on the role of the federal government and their influence on the process of providing funds for local social services. I sincerely hope these details hold your interest, because they provide a look at working relationships that you taxpayers fund but rarely get to inspect.

This story takes shape in chapter 3, with a broad overview of the homeless population, and a look at who is tasked with policy decisions and financial oversight for operation of services. It moves along to explain some of the changes that have occurred over the last 20 years, with some debate on the value of the most influential changes. Chapter 4 presents a summary of federal policy shifts that were underway and how they began to change the landscape of homeless services at the community level. In chapter 5, we will look back at the origin and history of Mather Community Campus, a homeless transitional housing program. Transitional housing was a common component of homeless services in many US cities in the early 2000s. Chapter 6 presents the federal policy shift away from transitional housing to the Housing First model. There is also a debate on the long-term value of the massive shift in federal funding alternatives and program design based on these policy changes. I hope to give the reader a thought-provoking look at the population we were attempting to serve and the organization of services that surrounded them for decades.

This is followed by a review of the resulting policy changes and how they changed the makeup of services available to the homeless. Before a summary of why these changes appear to be making the situation worse and the solutions harder to obtain, I attempt to recreate the experience of homeless clients who came to Mather Campus hoping for a new start. That section is presented to help the reader understand what has been lost in services to the homeless and why those things are critical. This book will also present financial data that impact local citizens, juxtaposed with the alternative uses for taxpayers' money that should be considered.

Included (in chapters 9 and 10) are true stories about a few special people whose lives were changed at Mather and their continuing impact on our community today. These are people who are still living in our community, yet their lives now are vastly different from what they imagined was possible while at the depths of their personal journeys. We'll take a look at what it took to change their lives. Please keep in mind, as we inspect the operation of homeless services in our community, the potential to create these success stories is disappearing.

All of us who worked and volunteered for the Mather program, and the clients who experienced its impact, are mourning deeply the closing of this program. It is improbable that we will ever see more comprehensive care for our homeless than was in the employment program at Mather Community Campus in Northern California. Losing this opportunity for our homeless citizens was a tragedy. But this book is not only about the Mather facility and the programs provided there. It is about the methods, the concept, the caring, and the scope of services that were in place there and the impact they had on the people who came through. It is about the loss of these services in our community and the loss of partnerships. The public and private partnerships that supported the program's objectives are gone now. It is also about how these changes can happen without a ripple of concern in the community. Finally, we hope to spark a conversation on how to go forward as a community to provide better care and opportunity for our unsheltered citizens.

This book is not about my religious beliefs, but those beliefs do inform my opinions. I am a minister at Volunteers of America ("the church without walls") and of course do believe in God. I am deeply motivated through His word. As a believer, I am motivated to live out my faith. That happens through my personal behavior and interaction with people. I have been working with our local homeless population through direct social service programming for the past 7 years and with organizations that have provided services to them since the year 2000. A large part of my motivation for doing this work comes from this foundational verse in the New Testament of the Bible:

> *Then the King will say to those on his right. "Come, you who are blessed by my Father, take your inheritance, the kingdom, prepared for you since the creation of the world. For I was hungry and you gave me something to eat, I was thirsty and you gave me something to drink, I was a stranger and you invited me in, I needed clothes and you clothed me, I was sick and you looked after me, I was in prison and you came to visit me." Then the righteous will answer him. "Lord when did we see you a stranger and invite you in, or needing clothes and clothe you. When did we see you sick or visit you in prison?" The King will reply, "I tell you the truth, whatever you did for one of the least of these brothers of mine, you did for me" (Matthew 25:34–40, NIV).*

CHAPTER 1

What Is the Point?

THIS IS A TRUE STORY ABOUT HOMELESSNESS AND HOME-less services. It is amazing how the truth can seemingly change with the perspective of those who hold it, tell it, or hear it. A very important objective of this work is to provide real information for the reader to think about—information that can be coupled with the related data to show the gravity of the situation caused by changes in the federal homeless policy.

This book is intended to make a point about what has been lost to the homeless population in our community and in many other places, for reasons that are difficult to explain. This work is *not* intended to provide THE answer to ending homelessness; but looking at what has been lost could be critical to developing better solutions for the future.

The advertising media today is flooded with messages that encourage our young citizens to "reach for the stars"; to not set limits on their expectations; and to "just do it." It is hard not to be motivated and enthused about this messaging and the potential impact it has on our children. But many children, teenagers, and young adults are not in a situation to receive these messages and pursue their dreams. For some children, their parenting, their environment growing up, or exposure to childhood trauma might exclude them from believing in a future with unlimited opportunity. Experience has taught us that many who end up homeless share that history. What was missing was not the opportunity itself. What was missing were the conditions to hear those messages, the vision to see where they can lead, and the support to "just do it."

There are always going to be people who will miss or pass on opportunity, for reasons that can be difficult to comprehend. Our responsibility as fellow members of the human race should be to make sure the door for opportunity stays open. We are supposed to be a country of second chances. How should we treat those who didn't get the tools early in life to explore their opportunities? How should we treat those who were living out "the good life" and then suffered serious setbacks that were out of their control? How about those who just made mistakes along the way?

We have made progress in this country on working toward equality for many ethnic and community groups, but it has taken decades, and there still remains underlying mistrust on all sides— this translates to missed opportunities. Most mistrust comes from not understanding the perspective of the persecuted. The homeless remain at the bottom of the barrel. This is not so much an ethnic issue but a social issue. The sobering truth about homelessness is that it does not discriminate against race, age, gender, or religion. Of course, other forms of discrimination place certain groups at higher risk to become homeless at some point.

Whatever leads people to become homeless, the silent majority in every community continues to discriminate against them. The discrimination comes in the form of not caring enough to lift a hand. These are not intentional acts of harm but a thoughtless distancing, which in some cases feel worse. Mother Teresa wrote in her book *In the Heart of the World*, "I have come more and more to realize that it is being unwanted that is the worst disease that any human being can ever experience." The homeless do not possess the same rights as others, and their path to equal rights is growing narrower, not broader like it should. The long-term consequences of this reality could lead to the rise of serious social, economic, and health-related problems in our communities.

As we have recently seen, across our nation, people are willing to stand up and protest against the needless killings of minorities by a few bad actors who have been entrusted with the authority to hand out "justice" as they see fit. Our country can be torn apart for extended periods by the loss of one life in that type of situation; and there is justification for it. But how do we let thousands of lives get wasted and often ended, day after day, year after year, without a ripple of public protest or meaningful action? Throughout 2020, we saw a movement of influential people in our country using their platforms to speak out about equality. The message is that all Americans deserve the same opportunity. Is that message intended to include the homeless?

The average citizen knows very little about the homeless population. They see what they see and make assumptions about character and intent without any real knowledge of an individual. This is the very foundation of implicit bias. How many times have you seen people with all their belongings in a shopping cart, or living in a tent under a freeway overpass, or sleeping on a park bench? There are even more people sleeping in cars, abandoned buildings, and fields. Are they considered brothers and sisters of our community?

When we skip that whole step of getting to know who we are assessing, we invariably reach bad and often reckless conclusions. I know I did before I started interviewing people who had been on the street for any significant time. If your assessment of the homeless comes only from seeing a few people holding signs on a street corner that say something like "Will work for food" or simply "I'm hungry," it may be hard for you to understand. These are human beings; every one of them is wonderfully made, and each person has a unique story that led them to where they are standing. Sure, there may have been some bad choices, but almost never with the willful intent of ending up homeless on the street.

This is a good place to pause and take a look at the history of one person who spent much of his life in and out of homelessness, one whom we eventually served as a client. This person was costing the county and the state thousands of dollars year after year. He was also costing businesses and citizens thousands of dollars—probably a staggering toll over his 10 to 12 years in the system. We will never know the true amount because so much of his struggle started before he became an adult and before he was being counted as homeless in our system. He first became a technically homeless adult in early 2007 and stayed in that category for 2 years, even though he had been homeless several other times. His financial impact on the community began at least a decade prior. For most of his early life, he was doing the only thing he had been prepared to do: survive. Read this story carefully. It is a gift from the individual who agreed to share it. It was very difficult for him to sit with me and recount much of this story. His name will remain confidential, but this story is true and real by every measure.

The need to preserve the possibilities for mistreated, forgotten, and less fortunate people was an essential reason for writing this book. From where I sit, the homeless remain the most disrespected and uncared for population in our country. But the human spirit, when treated with kindness and respect for its potential, can fuel the drive to change the course of a life. This man now gives the credit to God for the sustaining changes that have continued to keep him on his current path.

CHAPTER 2

Meet Jack:
A Redemption Story

DISCLOSURE: THE NAME HAS BEEN CHANGED TO PROTECT the privacy of this individual. That is the only change to this remarkable story, which honestly cannot capture the raw emotion I felt hearing it or the intensity of the struggle he lived with from an early age. I spent 3½ hours taking notes as fast as I could, only stopping to ask questions for clarity. Jack could write his own book, but in these next few pages I attempt to capture the most important points. Our meeting, at his request, started with a prayer.

Jack's earliest recollection of life as a child does not include any memories of his mother. As his story unfolded, there did not appear to be any moments that included the emotional and physical mother/child bonding that comes with being held and nurtured as an infant. Psychiatrists will tell you that is an essential component for developing psychological security. He wonders now if there was serious postpartum depression with his mother that never was addressed. But for whatever reasons, Mom was absent and Jack grew up in his father's house along with his maternal sister, who was

4 years older than he. He had an older stepsister who did not live with them.

Jack's father was not lacking for money. He held a very good job as a technician working on sophisticated equipment and used his earnings to buy a home, multiple boats, and a camper, and to live a reckless life. In those early years as a child, Jack remembers staying with his mother only a couple of times. She would treat her children like strangers, devoid of emotion and refusing to even share ice cream or soft drinks with them. Jack believes this dysfunctional relationship with his mother and the feelings it brought out led to a lifelong distrust of females. "Why would I trust someone with my deepest emotions who would just take them and leave?" he explained.

Jack's dad was a serious alcoholic. Jack told me his dad never let parenting interrupt his drinking. His dad's home was always being remodeled and was never finished. Growing up, neither he nor his sister ever got to sleep in their own bedrooms. They slept in the dining room, and the door to the family bathroom was covered only with a shower curtain. Jack would comment in retrospect how thoughtless and unkind that was to his older sister, to make her go her entire childhood and teenage years without a bathroom door. Despite the fact that the dad made a good living, not much of that ended up being shared with his children. They owned a washing machine but no dryer, because of the extra utility costs. Jack's dad would refuse to give him money for school lunches (80 cents a day) in favor of making him a lunch to take. The typical lunch was hot dogs cut in half and put between two pieces of bread and placed in a grocery bag. Jack, being too embarrassed to bring a lunch like that to school, would toss them in the garbage and go without rather than face the humiliation of his peers.

Jack's dad was a big man at the bar. He would loan money to almost anyone who needed it and would often buy a round of drinks for everyone when he got drunk. Jack's father was not physically abusive, but he was intolerant of Jack's mistakes and would hit him open handed across the forehead when he did disappoint his father. Dad was rigid and believed in being independent. He told Jack that he wasn't going to amount to anything. "If you want it done right, do it yourself," he would say. Before he left our interview, Jack told me that all he ever wanted from his father was his approval.

Every weekday, Jack's dad would come home from work at 3:30 p.m. Jack and his sister would hear him pull up and wait to see if he told them to get in the car. If he didn't, he would go straight to the bar, and Jack's older sister would watch him. Their father went to the same neighborhood bar every day. Once in a while, he would tell them to get in the car. He would then drive them to a friend's home to leave them there with that family. Those friends, who became known as their aunt and uncle, had their own children, including an older son. There were many nights that Jack and his sister would be left waiting alone at home for their dad to return from the bar drunk, or they would be waiting at the friends' house for him to pick them up. "I can't tell you how many white-knuckle rides home we had at 2:30 a.m. with our drunk father as small children."

The emergency phone number that Jack and his sister had for their father was the number to his regular bar. Jack told me there were nights he was scared and would call his father. Someone at the bar would pick up the phone and Jack would ask to speak to his father. He would hear the person who answered the phone holler his dad's name and say, "Your kid is on the phone." Many times, he heard the answer come back: "Tell him I'm not here," and then the phone would go dead. Other times they would tell him, "Your dad will pick up in a minute," only to have no one come to the phone and then have someone else just hang it up in 10 minutes or so. One evening, while staying at his "aunt's" house, Jack was sexually molested by the family's teenage son after he had lain down to sleep. Frantic, he went to tell the boy's mother. She pointed a finger at Jack and said her son would never do a thing like that and don't you ever repeat that lie again. Jack held that secret for 25 years; he was 7 years old.

Jack's dad continued to drink and began accumulating DUIs. He eventually would have to serve jail time. In seventh grade, Jack starting cutting school. He only attended classes for about 2 months that year. In eighth grade, he was sent to a continuation school. By the time he turned 12 years old, he was a runaway. He was now living on the streets or staying with relatives or friends of relatives. He stayed with his sister's best friend during part of this time. She took him in and treated him well. But he didn't adjust well because he had spent too much time on the street by that time. He left there to live with another family on and off for a couple of years: a family with four boys who were close in age. Because he was out of school for so long, Jack had developed too much anxiety, fear, and shame to return. He was now living with the reality that at 12 years old, there wasn't a soul on the planet looking for him. No parents, relatives, school officials, or anyone else who cared where he was living or how he was doing. For a short time, he hung around with a friend whose family accumulated cases of stolen beer. Jack's first experience with alcohol was drinking warm stolen Budweiser out of cans in a friend's closet. The beer was 4 years old. He was twelve.

While he was in eighth grade he stayed with his older stepsister, who was clean. She believed that her husband and her two stepsons were clean as well, a belief that turned out to be false. Her husband was a closet drug user, and the two boys were involved in dealing drugs. They took Jack to a local "dope house," where a young woman introduced him to methamphetamine. Jack was 13 years old at this time. The impact was immediate and dramatic. Jack felt invincible. In his words, he was high for 5 days. The boys asked him if he would like to learn how to work on cars. Jack said sure, and before he became aware of what he was getting into, he was helping to strip down stolen vehicles. Jack continued to use meth and hang out with these boys. A few years later, as a young teenager, Jack got arrested and placed in juvenile hall, also known as a neighborhood detention center. In his own words, "I was not sure how I got there."

In order to get released from juvenile hall, Jack had to contact a relative. With his father in jail, there was no one he could call, so he called his dad's friend, the same friend who had watched him when he was child the evenings his dad was at the bar. By pure circumstance, Jack's real aunt was in from Washington visiting this friend and agreed to come get him. She picked him up and took him back to the same house where he had been molested as a child. Full of anxiety, as soon as the adults weren't looking, Jack immediately split and went back to the streets. Shortly after this, Jack ended up at his deceased grandfather's house. His mother's brother was living there and he met his older cousin for the first time. The cousin was part of a gang that was dealing drugs and guns and stealing cars.

By now, Jack was using meth again. He soon became an integral part of the gang and was an expert at stealing cars, breaking into storage containers, and stealing unattended goods from cars and truck beds. Because he was a skinny young kid, they had him sliding under cracked garage doors and then opening them up fully so the other gang members could haul off the goods. The stolen goods were swapped for cash and drugs from a father of one of the gang members, who was the dope connection. At one point, Jack stayed up with no sleep for 16 days straight in a meth-induced psychosis. Jack was getting around twenty dollars a night for stealing thousands of dollars in goods. But he was an important man in this gang. Jack ended up spending years in this cycle.

Grand theft auto (GTA) got Jack back into juvenile hall. Jack's father was out of prison, on parole, when Jack was released to him and moved into a fifth-wheel trailer in his father's backyard. His dad was still remodeling the house, and there were no rooms that were usable. Jack was on probation and his father was now on parole. Both were required to attend Alcoholics Anonymous (AA) meetings and Jack was also attending Narcotics Anonymous meetings. But Jack's dad was dropping him off at the meetings and then going on to the bar. One day his father didn't show up after a meeting to pick him up. Jack called the same phone number, etched in his brain from childhood, to the bar and talked his father into picking him up. Part of Jack's probation required him to return to school, so Jack took classes to work toward his General Educational Development (GED) credential and got it in 2 months, to the absolute shock of his father. He accomplished this despite having not attended school regularly since the sixth grade.

On Jack's eighteenth birthday, after clearing his final drug test, he got off probation. He left his dad's house for the last time and went to live with a friend of his mother. The friend ran a very controlled meth business and used the money to invest in other legitimate businesses. Over the next few years, Jack would be arrested for GTA on four more occasions and would start serving jail time. He ended up spending time in seven different prisons, continuing to run, use drugs, and steal cars. He eventually ended up in Folsom Prison, where he spent 30 months. Over the years, because he hated people who drank and couldn't hold their liquor, he was in a lot of fights that generally ended up with Jack hurting someone. This behavior continued in prison, and before long Jack become a "level four" prisoner. This category of prisoners was excluded from the chow hall and had their movement in and out of their cells controlled and restricted. These were bad people. There were racial tensions in the prison, and during one small lapse of security Jack witnessed a brutal murder of one of the members of his group. It was his wake-up call that something had to change; he had to get out of that prison and never come back.

In between his times in jail, Jack managed to get two different women pregnant. Both presented him with the news while he was serving time. As the time approached for Jack's release from prison, he began to send out letters to drug treatment programs, hoping secure a bed immediately upon release. He knew without serious help he couldn't survive on the street for 1 day without getting high again. Everyone turned him down except for one program that, on his last and final request, offered him a bed. He began his substance abuse recovery in earnest at that program, another program that has since been closed.

At that time, Jack's prospects for starting a new life were not very good. He was in his early twenties and just beginning the long, up-hill battle of drug recovery. He was still suffering from the same anxiety that had alienated him his entire life. He still had a deep-seated emotional distrust of women. He had a serious criminal record and was covered with tattoos that identified him as a dangerous person. He was carrying the intense anger of untreated childhood trauma from the sexual abuse. He had no family to lean on at all. By this time, his father had sold his home and moved out of state and was dying from liver disease. Jack had no formal training that could lead to a decent job and had no experience to put on a resume. He had two children with different mothers, both of whom expected his financial and parental assistance. Who in the world would be willing to take a chance on this individual?

The events that helped Jack go from a level-four inmate in a maximum-security prison to where he is today are miraculous. There were many small things that helped him turn his life around.

It might be easy to dismiss any one of them as insignificant by itself; but Jack knows, and those of us who worked in these environments know, that many issues have to be dealt with and many hurdles cleared. They require the help and trust of your peers, your program staff, and your mentors in order to get through. Jack knows this better than anyone, and he expressed it in our interview. His story is truly remarkable, but there are hundreds more that are incredible in their own right; stories of people who overcame incredible odds and still managed to pull themselves up to a place of dignity and respect. The rest of his story, including his time at Mather, is presented in chapter 8, with several other clients' stories.

It is important to add here for further elaboration that not everybody who showed up at Mather Campus left completely rehabilitated, found employment, and rose up to become a solid contributor in the community. There were some who failed and drifted off to a different destiny. But there were so many more who made it out for good and left with their pride and the pride of all who knew them.

CHAPTER 3

Hope on the Run

ARE WE SYSTEMATICALLY ABANDONING THE FUTURE OF our homeless people without disclosure or public discussion? Looking at recent changes to homeless services in our communities and how they will impact our future, the answer in my opinion is *yes!* The homeless individual appears to be the most disenfranchised, disregarded, and unloved population in society, particularly in the United States. The more cynical may suggest that they are there by choice and are not disregarded at all. Some may also proclaim that we are spending millions of dollars on "those people" and that those resources could be put to more productive use elsewhere.

When I announced to friends and colleagues that I wanted to write this book, the question I most often heard was, "what do you hope to accomplish?" My answer is that I want people in our community and in other communities to have more information on what has changed in the design of homeless services, and why I believe we are now headed down a perilous path with the current system of care and the pending future planning. I also feel it is critically important for our community to have a better understanding of who makes up the homeless population and their potential for constructive change.

Identifying the Problem

The current system is dehumanizing a very large group of people who may never have an opportunity to know the pride that comes with self-sufficiency. These are individuals who have no experience with being part of a community, workforce, neighborhood, or family where people support and care for each other and then pass it on.

We need to examine the system and the officials whom we have entrusted with vast resources and important decisions on policies related to the growing epidemic of homelessness. Many are not only under-qualified but are in far over their heads. I am not talking about their individual intelligence or character, I am talking about the scope of work and the political pressure to solve the highest profile issues of the day. Homelessness should be at the top of any list. The things that make it extremely difficult, if not impossible, to solve, are the time, the resources, and the vision required to truly make a difference. We need leaders in our community, from multiple disciplines, to become immersed in collaborative, long-term problem solving. If we don't start soon, we may be looking at enormous social, economic, and civic unrest; all of which has historically led to rioting in the streets. That might sound dramatic, but again history shows that serious social unrest begins when the distance between the "haves" and the "have-nots" is unbridgeable and when people are persecuted for long periods of time.

We can't continue the current process of placing human beings, who are struggling to overcome multiple physical and mental health issues, into spaces that are not equipped to support long-term living, without providing the compliment of services necessary to keep them stable. We are already seeing some homeless rapid rehousing programs begin to produce slums and slumlords. How easy is it to forget when it comes to these situations that we are talking about fellow members of the human race? Some might try and tell you that many of them have chosen to "drop out" on their own and therefore no longer qualify to be a part of the community. Do not believe that this statement applies to all homeless people.

This negative profiling does not come from anyone who has worked with the homeless for many years. I sincerely wish I could share more of the stories that made up the population at Mather. Truly amazing people showed up there and worked their tails off. Almost every one of them showed up with the same goal: "I want to be a contributing member of my community." It is critical to note that while all of the services at Mather were essential to their chance at success, the game changer for virtually every client was eventually securing a job. When people have been homeless for extended periods of time, they lose their self-respect, the respect of others, and their sense of value. Going back to work, in virtually any capacity, immediately begins the process of reinstating those intangibles. There were many things required to get most ready to go to work, but employment was the final difference maker.

In his book *How to Be an Antiracist*, author Ibram Kendricks[1] refers to several sophisticated studies that compared the overall crime rate of individuals to unemployment rates. These studies were able to correlate rises in crime rates directly to rises in unemployment rates. Those studies could not correlate higher crime rates to any other criteria, including race. I mention this because employment became the "way out" for virtually all of our clients at Mather. In

---

1   Ibram Kendricks, *How to Be an Antiracist* (New York: Random House, 2019).

addition to creating the first step toward self-sufficiency, it also began to reestablish self-respect and the understanding that they were an important part of something bigger.

There Are No Shortcuts

Don't be fooled by recent headlines that suggest we can spend our way out of the homeless problems. You are being told that the problem is affordable housing. If we could just eliminate the supply problem and produce plentiful affordable housing, we can get this homeless problem under control. This is not only a false statement, but there is no historical or scientific data to support the claim. The closest historical comparison I can make is the current prison system in the United States. All we have to do is build more prisons, we were told. How well has that program worked? You might be thinking that this comparison overstates the problem too, but we will look much closer at what makes them similar.

By now we should know better; it is difficult to see the long-term positive results that justify why we continue to rely on politicians and government leaders to provide solutions to this complex problem. My personal observations indicate that government-run programs have produced very limited success to warrant our confidence and the unchecked use of our money. Let's take a look at the most powerful motivators for those in government. Politicians are motivated by power, driven by influential constituents, and ultimately have to bend to the high-pressure issues of the day. Many issues are driven purely by individual political motivations. If you need more proof, look at the inconsistency, from state to state, on the handling of the COVID-19 pandemic. Long-term strategies by politicians only cover the length of time to their next election.

Politicians will not solve the problems of homelessness in their 4- or 8-year terms. They rely on people who seek government jobs for the higher-than-average wage per experience level than the private sector, the higher-than-average benefit package than the private sector, and an extremely lucrative pension program that is fully funded and available after only 20 years. This is certainly true and widely recognized in California at the local, state, and federal level. In that environment, creativity is dangerous because it may push an individual to the edge or over their competency level (certainly their comfort level) and put their pension at risk. The longer an individual works for their local, state, or federal government, the more adverse they will become to the risks that are the product of ingenuity. That does not mean there can't be flashes of brilliance that bubble up far enough to become innovative programs; that probably happens more than we know. The problem is that the only thing more difficult than creating ingenuity in that environment is sustaining it long-term.

There are always exceptions. A handful of very ingenious people deserve praise, including the county employees who had a vision for truly unique homeless services in Sacramento County, California. They developed programming that was forward thinking, complex, compassionate, and dynamic in its design and roll out. The program provided unmatched opportunity for homeless singles and families for almost 20 years, winning two presidential awards for excellence. It has now been dismantled and closed—terminated for reasons that are almost impossible to comprehend but ones that fit perfectly into the description of the government culture I just described. Putting the effort into sustaining this program would have required challenging the new federal guidelines, and that was never a consideration.

An additional thought is this: leaders who make critical policy decisions that impact people's lives without ever having spent a day in their shoes are likely to miss the mark. They skip the step of intimately meeting the people and understanding their motivations, their needs, and their potential. Skipping this step will usually guarantee disservice to those people. *Those people* is an appropriate term to use in telling this story. I've heard it many times in reference to the homeless in our community. Most often it was followed with a list of adjectives and adverbs that were meant to dehumanize and disparage "those people."

The homeless remain a large, still growing, and for the most part, misunderstood segment of our population. There do not appear to be many who are willing to stand up and support enhancing the future for these people. We hope to correct, on a large scale, the shortsighted perceptions of the population as a whole. I know as well as anyone that in every community there are a few individuals, for a variety of reasons, who cannot or choose not to contribute. It is impossible to judge why an individual is capable of achieving certain results; this is also true within the homeless population. The percentage of the homeless population that just choose to "opt out" is much smaller than most people believe and is probably close to the norm for all populations.

There may be some in the government sector, tasked with funding and monitoring local social service programs, who will attempt to discredit much of what you are going to read in this book. They may say that the data do not support the claims. I have two rebuttal points for the reader to keep in mind. (1) Data can be manipulated to create different story lines. I have watched this tactic used for years to support current political policy when it comes to the homeless. (2) Certain facts are irrefutable, no matter how the data are presented. They come in the form of anecdotal information that is connected to the real-life experiences of many people. I am hoping that many of the people who were touched by their experience of leaving homelessness will validate this work and maybe, just maybe, help create a better opportunity for the thousands still struggling to put homelessness behind them for good.

You can make up your own mind on how we should proceed as a community with our brothers and sisters who are homeless after you read this book. You hear one side of the story virtually every day, in the newspaper or on television. I hope to provide some new insights and revelations that might be new to you as you read through this book.

CHAPTER 4

A Brief on Recent Changes to Homeless Services

FOR THE PURPOSE OF THIS REVIEW, THE TIME FRAME "RECENT" is defined as the years 2000 to 2020. The regional care model represented in this narrative is from Northern California. Because the most significant changes in the approach to solving the homeless problem in this country have been top-down federal policy changes, it doesn't really matter what part of the country is being reviewed, the story will not drastically change. The fact that we support our politicians as they continue, decade after decade, to institute one-size-fits-all policies in a nation based on the inalienable rights of individuals is mind-numbing. Our founding fathers wrote the Federalist Papers (the "how to" book for managing a democracy) with the specific intent of controlling this kind of power at the federal level.

My Background

To give you some background on where my views on homeless care originated, the following is an abbreviated history of my time in social services. Late in my professional career (January 2014), I stepped into the actual work of serving the homeless population as an employee of Volunteers of America, a nonprofit social services provider. I had served on their board of directors for the previous 8 years and stepped down to take the position. Prior to that, I was an executive for 30 years for two different national homebuilders. My first experience with social service providers came through my affiliation with the local homebuilding association in Northern California. We created a builder-based nonprofit organization. Our mission was to partner with local social service providers on a number of community service improvement projects designed to provide additional transitional beds for homeless populations. This is where I met the people at Volunteers of America. We worked together on making improvements to a number of homeless program facilities over a period of 6 years before I was asked to serve on their board. By then, I had spent almost 15 years, on the perimeter, learning about homeless services and occasionally engaging with homeless individuals. My early perceptions of this population began to change in 2014 when I accepted a position as the program director for the employment program at Mather Community Campus.

Distribution of Homeless Services

This work is being written with the hope it can benefit the entire homeless population. It is helpful to understand how the population is separated for public services. Not all homeless people get equal treatment or equal allocation of resources in the world of social services. I am certain that does not come as a surprise. There are basically three client categories for homeless service distribution: families, youth/foster youth (18 to 24 years old), and single adults. There are some additional nuances within these categories, but these create the basic population split for segregating locations and services. Over the years, public funding, breadth of services, and the ability to attract community support and private funding have favored homeless families first. The youth and former foster youth population is a close second, and the singles population has remained in a distant last place. Most citizens feel that these individuals have just made a lot of bad choices along the way. They feel they are not necessarily good people and that many remain homeless by choice. They are expected at some point to pull themselves up by their bootstraps and move on. Right or wrong (and it is mostly wrong), this has been their history. It may not come as a surprise, but single adults make up the largest segment of the homeless population. We need major changes in policy for the benefit of all of our homeless, but this group was a huge motivator to write this book.

Mather Community Campus (MCC) was an employment-based transitional housing program that was a part of a regional Continuum of Care (COC) for homeless services in the Sacramento region. The COC included a significant number of public and private social service providers. MCC was designed with the objective to exit people from homelessness, permanently, through an employment to housing program. For many years, the Sacramento County Department of Human Assistance was the agency that facilitated the flow of federal, state, and local funds for these services through contracts with service providers. The county oversaw the processes and procedures for the use of these funds through their contract monitoring system. Over time, an organic referral system emerged among area service providers for moving homeless people into different service levels that ultimately led many to MCC.

Like most counties in California and the United States, the structured entry points for people experiencing homelessness in Sacramento are the individual and family shelters. Shelters are intended for short stays, and prior to the federal policy changes, the shelter providers could refer clients out to other service providers who they felt could further benefit their individual client. If there were people struggling with addictions, they could be referred to an alcohol and drug recovery program. If there were mental health issues, they could be referred to an appropriate treatment program. If they were released prisoners, under parole or probation, the shelter could work with appropriate law enforcement to navigate a logical next step for their clients. Most of these providers referred their clients to the employment program at Mather Community Campus when they felt they were ready. This program was recognized to create the best opportunity for clients to leave homelessness permanently.

In this system, a homeless individual could go from the street to a shelter, and then because of alcohol and drug problems, be referred to a recovery facility. After an appropriate period of stabilization, they might then be referred to Mather, where it was expected that sobriety would be maintained through rigorous programming, including regular drug testing and recovery groups. The idea then was that the individual could work through any other barriers to employment at Mather, where they could also get pre-employment and vocational training and eventually be placed in a job. This would ultimately allow them to save money and move into their own place. The same process could start with a parole or probation agent or a mental health facility. On the occasions where clients would relapse or regress, they could be relocated for a period of time to a program that could address that specific issue and then reapply to MCC when appropriate. Mather became a coveted destination for many of the homeless staying in shelters or rehabilitation programs. Over the years, a waiting list developed for those who wanted to be referred to this program. There were months when the wait list grew to over 200 people.

Mather remained the recipient of federal funding through HUD, in addition to other county funding that came through a number of different agencies. The program clients were eligible to receive additional cooperative services from other agencies that were captured as in-kind financial support each year. This system worked flawlessly, from my perspective, for the first 3 years that I was the director (2014–2017). Additionally, from all the research I have done with the previous Mather directors, it had worked just as well since opening in 1996, when people were first enrolled. Thousands of clients were served, and thousands left homelessness behind through this program.

Change in Federal Policy

Toward the end of the George W. Bush administration and during the early stages of the Obama administration, the philosophy concerning funding homeless services at the federal level had changed dramatically. By 2014, legislation that had passed in 2009 would change the direction of the US Department of Housing and Urban Development (HUD) regarding its role in homeless services. Basically, new policy would restrict HUD funding only to programs that led directly to the inclusion of new housing units. There would be no more HUD funds available to pay for "supportive services." I recall sitting in a large conference room in Washington, DC, during the annual National Alliance to End Homelessness conference. I was listening to the number-two man at HUD make the announcement that HUD had been spending $1.5 billion dollars on the homeless in the nation. He noted that almost $500 million of that total was spent on supportive services. He then went on to say that HUD would no longer fund supportive services and would instead use that $500 million to increase the supply of housing

35

options. The reasons given to support this change were two fold. First, HUD was a housing agency, not a service provider. Second, their belief was that these additional housing units would do more to end homelessness than the money being spent on services. That statement ended up totally missing the mark. He told the service providers in the room to go find their money for supportive services someplace else.

This was the beginning of the end of transitional housing (and most of the services that were a part of those programs). Transitional housing programs had been one of the HUD-funded staples for homeless programs in most major metropolitan areas for years. If there were any questions about the future of transitional housing, the HUD director announced at that same conference that HUD was going to stop funding transitional housing programs in the near future. What was coming down the tracks for homeless services was a new homeless service model, supported by new independent research and modeling. The new model was called Housing First.

The Housing First Model

Before I go on to talk about the systematic dismantling of transitional housing and the race to ubiquitous "housing first," I feel obligated to make this statement: *I believe there is a very valuable place for Housing First models in a structured Continuum of Care system.* Having said that, I have learned to be wary of any one-size-fits-all approach to any social issue in our country. That approach never works. In this particular case, I had a few years of working in a program that had incredible success to enforce my certainty that a total move away from transitional housing was going to create missed opportunities for large numbers of our homeless population, regardless of how this change was implemented. Some of that was speculation at the time based on what I thought I knew. Now it is absolute certainty backed by real evidence, real data, and real life in our community.

Housing First is a homeless service model that is today the preferred model in most communities in the United States. When I say, "preferred," I mean it is the one model remaining that has the most access to federal, state, and county funding streams. Funding sometimes creates preferences that are not fully backed by results. But since federal and state governments provide the major funding sources for social services in our country, service models are forced to follow federal funding guidelines.

Housing First is a relatively new model for human service programs and social policy for the treatment of people who are homeless.[2] It is an alternative to a system of emergency shelter/transitional housing progressions. That system moved homeless individuals through different levels of housing with services, where each level moved them closer to independent housing. Housing First moves the homeless individual or household immediately from the streets or homeless shelters into their own independent housing unit. Housing First approaches are based on the concept that a homeless individual or household's primary need is to obtain stable housing and that other issues that may affect the household can and should be addressed once housing is obtained.

Housing First is an approach that offers permanent, affordable housing placement as quickly as possible for homeless individuals and families.[3] Once housing is secured, light-touch case management

---

2   Wikipedia, "Housing First," https://en.wikipedia.org/wiki/Housing_First

3   United States Interagency Council on Homelessness, "Housing First," 2015, https://web.archive.org/web/20151210215638/

and voluntary engagement with other community support programs becomes the service model used to assist with keeping the client housed and not returned to homelessness. The principles are summarized below.[4]

1. Move people into housing directly from the street and/or shelters without preconditions of treatment acceptance or compliance.

2. The provider is obligated to bring robust support services to the housing. These services *are predicated on assertive engagement, not coercion.*

3. Continued tenancy *is not dependent on participation in services.*

4. Priority for units is targeted to the most disabled and vulnerable homeless members of the community first.

5. *Embraces a harm reduction approach to addictions rather than mandating abstinence.* At the same time, the provider must be prepared to support a resident's commitment to recovery.

6. Residents must have leases and tenant protections under the law.

---

4 United States Interagency Council on Homelessness, "Implementing Housing First in Supportive Housing," 2014. http://usich.gov/usich_resources/solutions/explore/housing_first/

7. Can be implemented as either a project-based or scattered site model.

The list presented above on Housing First principles could be successfully implemented for a significant group of the homeless. There are many of us working in social services that believe that if Housing First had been introduced as a new and separate service model, the impact could have been more positive. That would have required this program model to be added to the existing Continuum of Care system and supported with an effective triage system. Triaging is the process of determining the priority of an individual's treatment needs based on the severity of their condition or likelihood of recovery with or without treatment. This is important because the success of Housing First is contingent upon a person's ability to maintain their housing stability independent of outside support within a relatively short period of time. Within the homeless population, there is a high level of substance abuse that is often coupled with co-occurring levels of mental health issues and physical ailments. If these conditions are not treated, meeting all of the requirements to maintain independent housing is very difficult, if not impossible.

We will examine why the rush to implement Housing First, including the replacement of existing programs, set back our goals of ending homelessness. Our progress has been so arrested that it is hard to see when some credible, sustainable improvement might happen in the future. Housing First, in its current form and under the current direction from federal and state governments, is not capable of meeting the mark as a sole solution model for ending homelessness.

In chapter 6 we will take a closer look at the research and ensuing policy changes that led to the widespread adoption of the

Housing First model. But first let's examine the Mather transitional housing program that was defunded and dismantled as a result of the shift to Housing First. It is both stunning and disheartening to understand what has been unwittingly abandoned in services to homeless singles in such a short period of time.

CHAPTER 5

Mather Community Campus: The Vision and the Early Years

HERE IS THE ABRIDGED STORY OF THE CONCEPTUAL DESIGN and launch of Mather Community Campus, an employment-based, transitional housing program for homeless single adults and families. The many remarkable people who were there at the beginning deserve credit for the years of effort it took to open Mather in 1996. To begin, we will focus on the comprehensive program they built and on the people who were served. There are descriptions of the programming that was developed and what, we are certain now in retrospect, was the special blend of people skills and program parts that made it all work. The documents I researched go back to 1992. The staff and management I interviewed go back to 1996. This chapter is a consolidated look at the good fortune, forward thinking, and hard work many people contributed to get this program put together and opened.

How Mather Got Its Start

Mather Air Force Base was decommissioned from the military by the Clinton administration in the early 1990s. The thirty-three acres of property included utility buildings that had been used for a variety of purposes, including storage, administrative services, and a noncommissioned officer's club. There were twenty single-family bungalows, along with multiunit, multistory residential buildings that had been used for housing the Airmen and their families. There also was a very large warehouse and a library, which was converted later into a commercial kitchen and dining hall. The base had about fifteen acres of open space. When the federal government turned the facility over to Sacramento County, the Air Force certified the property as environmentally safe and retained the responsibility for any future civil engineering issues. The county arranged for a loan through Sacramento Housing and Redevelopment Agency (SHRA) to renovate the residential units to accommodate future county homeless residents. SHRA developed a regulatory agreement that mandated the property be used exclusively for homeless services for the next 50 years. The county agreed, and the renovations began.

Over the next few years, forward-thinking Sacramento County personnel, with input from nonprofit service agencies, collaborated on a plan to develop a transitional housing program for homeless singles and families at Mather. At the time, it was groundbreaking in its concept and design for providing homeless services. There were two hundred studio apartments with private bathrooms for the singles population (later referred to as the single site) that were to be serviced in the three-story buildings. The bungalows, which were abandoned later, were used initially to serve homeless families. There were another sixty one-, two-, and three-bedroom apartments with kitchens and bathrooms in the two-story buildings that would eventually (2005) serve the family program (referred to as the family site). The commercial kitchen and dining hall were to be used to serve the single site customers three hot meals per day and to become the gathering place for meetings that would include the entire community. Families were expected to prepare their own meals and have family mealtimes in their own apartments.

The program opened in 1996 as a 2-year transitional housing program designed to prepare and move homeless singles and families into independent living, through education, vocational training, barrier reduction, and employment. An office of the Sacramento Employment and Training Agency (SETA One-Stop) was planned for the campus, and after renovations, it opened in two of the utility buildings on site. (A One-Stop Career Center is a stand-alone county-run employment center.) Another utility building became the administrative offices for the single and family programs. An additional three utility buildings were converted into classrooms and a recreation center. The physical property was ready to begin programming.

The chosen name for these family and single homeless programs was Mather Community Campus. The naming of the site was important, as it was meant to establish a new paradigm for the people coming into the programs. First, the name "campus" created the feeling of a college community, not a homeless program. Second, the customers were to be referred to as "students." This not only supported the college campus environment, but just as important, it was a first step away from being referred to as homeless people.

The Original Team

The original team that put the finishing touches on the programming, funding, and design for the campus operations included the following groups:

- Sacramento County Department of Human Assistance (DHA);

- Sacramento Employment and Training Agency (SETA);

- Sacramento Housing and Redevelopment Agency (SHRA);

- Pride Industries;

- Next Move (formerly Sacramento Area Emergency Housing Center); and

- Volunteers of America, Northern California (VOA).

This was one of the first true collaborations anywhere in the United States that was designed to provide comprehensive services with the goal of moving a large number of people from homelessness to self-sufficiency. The original brain trust had thought through the needs and the process thoroughly, and although there would be reductions to the program later because of funding cuts, the basic service model remained intact for almost 20 years.

Initially, the Sacramento County DHA would be responsible for the overall operation of the program. This included the day-to-day management of all services, the intake process for customers, financial management, and the administrative services for the campus. They appointed a program director and hired the administrative personnel.

SETA had a team located at this new One-Stop, which was intended to serve Mather students as well as any local residents who were looking for help with finding jobs. SETA provided easy access to find jobs (through their regional jobs network) when an individual was ready to work. They also provided funding to Mather students for vocational training, work clothes, and certain light equipment needed for specific jobs. The staff at the One-Stop included DHA employees who were tasked with providing educational and vocational assessments for all new clients, and the eventual creation of an Individual Employment Plan for each of them. They also provided contacts for working on criminal record reduction and access to a program that allowed the students to get their driver's license reinstated (when necessary) for five dollars. SETA funds were also used to establish an incentive program for the Mather students.

Sacramento Regional Housing Authority provided the funding vehicle to renovate the residential units. They also provided a detailed outline on how to run a residential housing program, and were responsible for overseeing the regulatory agreement designating the facility as a program for homeless individuals. Over the years, they would continue to do annual inspections of the physical property and provide a list of necessary corrections and repairs to keep the facilities in good working order. In the early years, SHRA had crew at Mather for routine building maintenance.

Next Move was awarded the contract to provide case management for the families (adults and children). Volunteers of America was awarded the contract for the single site students to provide case management and later the food preparation service in the commercial kitchen. They were also responsible for other services, including credit repair and teaching life skill classes. Pride Industries was awarded the contract for employment services, with the responsibility to provide additional job opportunities for Mather students.

During the planning process, there was resistance from residents and staff at the City of Rancho Cordova to get the use permits needed to operate homeless services programming at Mather. Eventually, the parties agreed to approve the use plan. In an effort to be a part of regular continuing oversight, the city of Rancho Cordova and Sacramento County formed an advisory board, called the Community Action Committee (CAC board). This committee was composed of prominent Rancho Cordova citizens who would be provided quarterly updates on program outcomes at the "all-community" meetings held at Mather.

Initial Eligibility Requirements

When the campus opened, it was available to any homeless individual who met the eligibility requirements. There were clients who came directly to the program through the County Department of Human Assistance. Referrals would eventually come from alcohol and drug recovery programs, other homeless programs for singles and families, shelters, probation and parole, and other social service providers in the community. At one point, Mather had received referrals from more than sixty different agencies. For the better part of the period from the year 2000 through 2015, there were usually two to three hundred people on a waiting list hoping to get into Mather Campus.

There were a few mandatory eligibility requirements. First, you had to be homeless, per the regulatory agreement. The definition of who was considered homeless changed over the last 20-year period, but the profile of the people did not change in any significant way. Because there were children on campus, the county and the City of Rancho Cordova agreed that individuals with recent violent crimes (within 3 years) would not be eligible. Neither were individuals with any history of sex offenses. All others were welcome to apply. There was a written standard that stated one could not complete an application or enter the program if they tested positive "the day of" for alcohol or drug use.

The key component for being accepted at Mather was the willingness to seek employment. Individuals with disabilities were welcome, and staff would work to maximize disability benefits with the possibility of adding part-time employment. The people who really wanted to go to work usually succeeded in the program. New prospective clients came each week on Thursday morning. They would first get a tour of the campus and the facilities by a staff member and an explanation of the program requirements. Then they would fill out an application and some form of a resume, after completing drug testing. The applicants would be given lunch, and in the early afternoon they would interview with a team from the Mather and/ or DHA staff. After the interviews were completed, a member of each interview team would make a presentation and recommendation to the entire Mather staff on behalf of the applicant. There was usually robust discussion following the interviews on the pros and cons of the applicant. If they were accepted, their file would be given to the intake coordinator to do a background check that usually took 1 week. The client would be notified immediately of their acceptance after the background report was received and cleared. All new move-ins occurred on the Wednesday following approval notifications. The 10–15% who were not accepted during their initial interview were given a plan to follow to keep their option open to get into the program. Many were successful with their second or third application.

Once accepted, an individual was eligible for Mather benefits from the county, which paid for their housing and the services provided on the campus. They were also eligible for food stamps, bus passes, and access to a county grant that paid for vocational training, work clothes, and certain necessary work tools. They were assigned to their own studio apartment unit, with individual bathrooms, and were given a mailbox key for their space in the community mailbox system. There was always excitement and gratitude displayed by the students when they got the keys to their own apartment unit and mailbox. For many, it had been years since they had their own place and their own bathroom.

Sacramento County DHA, with support from the county Board of Supervisors, petitioned the federal government FDA food stamp program for permission to take the student's food stamps, in the singles program, each month to offset the cost of providing three hot meals per day, every day of the week. They were granted permission to do so, and the surrender of food stamps each month was part of the program for the students. When a student started working and lost their food stamp benefits (usually 5 to 8 weeks after the county received a copy of their first paycheck stub), they were required to pay the same amount for their meals, at the beginning of each month, out of their own income. The same was true with rental payments for their housing, which were capped at 30% of their income. Rental rates were capped at the maximum of market rate rent for an efficiency apartment in the area. The cost per meal over 20 years was somewhere between two and three dollars each. This transfer of financial responsibility served two purposes: The first was that it provided the student with step toward learning how to financially manage a household; the second was that it provided additional incentive to move into their own permanent housing.

New students were provided a safe place to live, rent free, along with three hot meals per day, a registered mailing address, and a small monthly stipend for personal items. They were now ready to begin the program. The years that I was responsible for reviewing student profiles showed remarkable consistency in their personal profiles and employment barriers. The percentage of our new students who had been struggling with alcohol or drug addictions was usually more than 80%; the percentage who came with existing criminal backgrounds was 70%. The average age was always between 40 and 44 years old. Mather would end up serving people from 18 to 70 years old, year in and year out. Virtually none of our clients came with an active bank account. Fewer than 10% had a driver's license and very few had completed high school. There was virtually no current work history, though there were some interesting resumes. Mather Community, when full, served every age, every gender, every religion, every sex, and every ethnicity. They came with some of the most difficult and heart-rending histories of growing up and entering adulthood that anyone could ever imagine. Either that, or they had experienced some traumatic event in their life that had changed their fortunes dramatically.

The Mather Program

When Mather Community Campus (MCC) had finally cleared all of the hurdles and opened for services in 1996, it was a 2-year transitional housing program. The program was designed to create a stable environment for homeless individuals and families where they could be sheltered and provided meals, and begin the work of preparing themselves to get employment. They would also need to save money to eventually move out of Mather and into their own apartment or home. The program design was about doing the things necessary to leave homelessness for good. The final tools were employment readiness and obtaining full-time employment. Even though the program allowed clients to stay up to a maximum of 2 years, they were encouraged to complete each segment as quickly as possible and to then start looking for work.

On move-in day all new residents signed a lodging agreement and the "Program Guidelines." Adherence to the program guidelines was a requirement of the lodging agreement, which could be terminated for noncompliance. The afternoon of the day they moved in, each client would meet with their case manager and complete a student profile sheet that gathered all of the information about their current circumstances. The case manager would then engage the student in some conversation about their expectations and the expectations of the MCC staff.

The first full day after moving in was spent completing educational and interest assessments that became the foundation of their Individual Service Plan and their Individual Employment Plan. Some of the students were eligible for continuing education, such as completing high school or a GED program or taking college courses. There were several students who applied for and received Pell Grants to take college courses during their first 6 to 12 months in the program. Outside of these optional program opportunities, there were requirements that all clients had to meet to remain in the program and to move forward. They included the following:

- Attend a group meeting with their case manager every week.

- Complete 196 hours of community service work.

- Complete 6 weeks of life skills and pre-employment training classes on site.

- Complete the 6-week "Ready to Rent" classes.

- Students with any prior substance abuse issues were required to attend a minimum of three AA meetings per week.

- Pass room inspection every Tuesday.

- Obey curfew and visitation policy.

- Attend the monthly "all-community" meeting (this was all about celebrating successes and hearing from former students who were succeeding in their new lives outside of MCC).

- Follow all other program guidelines.

Students who followed these requirements were then required to attend a 2-week "Job Club" training at the DHA location on campus. This was to learn resume preparation, job searching techniques, and sessions on how to interview with a potential employer for work. After completing Job Club, students could choose to begin looking for work or enroll in a variety of different vocational training courses.

Therapeutic Community

In reviewing the basic requirements that applied to all students, it is easy to miss the component of program design that had students working together in common classes on common issues. This included celebrating success together and holding each other accountable for doing their share and following program guidelines. The term associated with this form of collaborative learning and community responsibilities is *therapeutic community*. Without transitional housing programs, there is little opportunity to create a therapeutic community design for alcohol and drug recovery in homeless programs. The therapeutic community approach is still considered a valuable recovery treatment tool, according to the National Institute on Drug Abuse.[5] In the age of Housing First, we do not hear much about this practice. However, virtually everybody we interviewed, and there have been hundreds, who successfully finished the MCC program told us this was a critical element of their journey. Being part of a community where everyone was working toward common goals was an essential element of their success. Over the years, with the help of the students, a communal garden was developed to grow fresh vegetables for the kitchen. They also helped build a chicken coop that provided fresh eggs and hours of entertainment for the children on campus. Mather Community Campus became a fully functioning self-contained community.

Vocational Training

MCC had a variety of vocational training programs available for students on the campus itself. These programs changed with the market conditions over the years and as examples included the following:

- Culinary training (in the kitchen);

- Janitorial (on campus);

- Landscape maintenance (on campus);

- Building maintenance (on campus);

- Security guard training (off campus);

---

5 National Institute on Drug Abuse, "What Is a Therapeutic Community's Approach?" (2015, July), https://www.drugabuse.gov/publications/research-reports/therapeutic-communities/what-therapeutic-communitys-approach

- Certified nursing assistant training (off campus);

- Forklift driving (off campus);

- Truck driving, Class A license training (off campus);

- Smog tech certification (off campus).

Generally, vocational training programs required 3 to 4 months for completion and certification. These programs were very cost effective, with an average cost of only $1,500 to complete certifications.

Job Development and Employment

The Mather program had a full-time employment specialist who worked with the case managers to develop an Individual Employment Plan for each student. After completing the initial program elements, including vocational training if needed, they would enter the program element called Job Search. During this period, they would meet with the employment specialist to begin the search for work. A critical element of the employment specialist role was job development. This work was done through visiting local businesses to establish relationships with human resource managers and learn about their hiring practice. Twice a year the Mather team would host a job fair on the campus, where 20 to 35 businesses would come and set up displays about their companies and meet with students. For most of the students, it was a new experience to stand in front of a prospective employer and talk about who they were and what they wanted to do going forward.

Job fairs were generally followed up with hiring events on the Mather Campus for those companies that had multiple students interested in going to work for them. A new manufacturing company that was opening a facility in Folsom, California, and had multiple job openings attended one hiring event in 2014. Thirty-nine students showed up and completed applications and interviews; 34 of them were hired over the following month. All of these interactions with local businesses led to the development of more opportunities for the Mather students. The companies became invested in the success of the program as well as that of the clients.

Additional Program Components

There was a "benchmark" program that allowed each student to accumulate up to $450 for achieving certain milestones that was kept in an account in their name. Deposits were made for completing their community service hours, completing the required class work, and finally for getting a job. In order to collect the full amount at discharge, they had to complete all of the other program requirements and settle any debt prior to leaving. This element was funded through SETA as part of a community service block grant that also paid for the vocational training.

MCC staff included the following specialists: case managers to provide one-on-one counseling and assistance; a credit specialist who worked with students to repair or establish credit; a housing specialist who was responsible for maintaining an inventory of housing options for clients when they left; and a drug testing specialist who was responsible for notifying students of random drug testing appointments and then conducting those drug tests. MCC also had a licensed clinical social worker on staff who could help with counseling and alcohol and drug recovery issues, and who could provide certifications for disabilities. All the staff at MCC was involved in teaching the life skills and pre-employment classes.

MCC provided a rigorous experience for all who enrolled. Everyone had to work hard, 5 days a week for 6 to 8 months, to complete the basic program requirements. They would then have to complete vocational and pre-employment training and go find a job. All of this had to be done in order to put them in a position to move out into their own housing solution.

Thousands of people completed the Mather program between 1997 and 2019, with many of them exiting homelessness for good. The population fluctuated during the ramp-up period from 1998 to 2005. When fully operational, there were 180 singles on campus and 60 families, with an average of 130 children, totaling 370 residents. The campus operated at this level from 2005 through 2015, when the family population in the employment program began being reduced because of funding cuts. It was reduced to zero over a 2-year period. The singles population remained at 180 until 2017, when it was reduced to 140. The program accepted new clients every month, and existing clients finished the program and left every month. We averaged 15 to 20 completions each month for my 6 years of managing the singles. Because the average stay was 9 months, around 230 clients could finish each year. Because of fluctuations and because the county ran this program independently for 10 years without detailed population records, it is difficult to get an exact count on the total census served. Our best estimate is that in excess of four thousand people participated in the Mather program from start to finish. The independent counts on recidivism for Mather reported to the Continuum of Care and published each year was less than 5% annually, which was always the best of all programs reporting.

The Best Use of the Mather Property

For many years, those coming to Mather were almost exclusively referrals from dozens of different service providers, along with the offices of probation and parole. The Mather intake process only screened out people for violent backgrounds and sex offenses and accepted virtually all others who expressed a desire to go to work. These clients provided a representative mix of all homeless people in the county. Even after a year of working under HUD's coordinated entry requirement, with no consideration given to match candidates to programming, and with all of them coming from the list of the most vulnerable, almost 50% were still leaving with jobs and housing. Setting that aside, the simple argument locally is that there is a need, a real social responsibility, to find the highest and best use for the facilities that were given to the region to be used for homeless services—a property that is still governed by a regulatory agreement that requires it to be used for homeless services. Where else in our country is this story playing out with the loss of opportunity continuing to accrue to the homeless?

The employment to housing program was the use of Mather that most benefited the homeless clients and the community. *No one is suggesting that everyone experiencing homelessness will be able to come to a program like Mather and get a job and move into market housing. The argument is that everyone who can possibly achieve those objectives deserves the chance to have the opportunity.* The changes that have been made at Mather have permanently removed that opportunity from 180 to 200 people every year. We all agree that it is inevitable that many of the homeless will need permanent supportive housing. That is not a point being argued here either. The question being asked is, "What was the best use of the Mather campus facilities?" That best use was the transitional housing employment model, and it was reflected by the positive impact that it had on so many of the homeless in our community. It is further supported by the financial analysis of the use of taxpayers' resources. The continuing discussion should have focused on how to duplicate this service model in multiple locations. It is difficult to understand why these opportunities were never considered.

CHAPTER 6

Change in the Wind: Federal Mandates

AT THIS POINT, WE ARE MOVING AWAY FROM THE DISCUS-sion of the local homeless services models, including what was being offered at the Mather Campus in Northern California. All homeless services were about to be impacted by policy changes that were occurring at the federal level. There was a major shift in funding alternatives coming for service providers that was based on the research of the aforementioned new service model: Housing First. We will first explore that model in more depth, including the positive and negative views that have surfaced over the last 10 years. We will then circle back and look at how this shift in policy changed everything about the way services to the homeless would be organized in the future and how those programmatic changes and their associated funding changes impacted both those in need of services and those providing services.

A Deeper Look at Housing First

It is essential to reiterate here that there is an important place for Housing First programs in a continuum of care for homeless services in our community today. This is not an argument against the philosophy or the practical and intelligent implementation of those programs. As stated, however, I strongly argue against this being a one-size-fits-all model that adequately serves the needs of all who are trying to exit homelessness. Below is a short history of some of the early programming and research that eventually led to this dramatic shift in federal funding.

The Case for Housing First

In Los Angeles in 1988, the Housing First program for families was launched at Beyond Shelter by Tanya Tull in response to a sharp increase in the number of homeless families with children.[6,7] The Housing First approach for families included in-depth screening and assessment for child safety. In Housing First for families, services are available before, during, and after relocation to rental housing, *but engagement in those services is not a requirement for participation*. Unfortunately, the Housing First philosophy was often misinterpreted in later years, and today many government programs promote faulty application of Housing First. For households with children, appropriate services and monitoring may be delivered through home visits, outpatient treatment, or linking to appropriate services in the community at large.[8]

6　Ashoka, "Tanya Tull, Ashoka Fellow," 2009, https://www.ashoka.org/en-us/fellow/tanya-tull

7　Partnering for Change, "About Beyond Shelter," https://www.partnering-for-change.org/about-beyond-shelter/

8　National Alliance to End Homelessness, "Organizational Change: Adopting a Housing First Approach," 2009, https://endhomelessness.org/resource/organizational-change-adopting-a-housing-first-approach/

In 1992, Dr. Sam Tsemberis, a faculty member of the Department of Psychiatry at New York University School of Medicine, founded Pathway to Housing in New York City. His philosophy was that Housing First for the chronically homeless should be premised on the notion that housing is a basic human right and so should not be denied anyone, *even if they are abusing alcohol or other substances.* The Housing First model is philosophically in contrast to models that require the homeless to abjure substance abuse and seek treatment in exchange for housing.[9]

In 1996 a paper based on the principle of critical time intervention was published through the Columbia School of Medicine. This principle was studied for its effectiveness in preventing recurrent homelessness among severely mentally ill men after their discharge from a shelter. A total of 96 men were included in the study, and there were two groups tested in a clinical trial. One was the critical time intervention (CTI) group and the other was the usual services only (USO) group.[10] The CTI group was placed in independent housing with intense wraparound services, while the USO group continued to get the usual transition services as they transitioned to community living. During the first 3 months, the CTI group had support from social workers who made regular home visits, met with caregivers, and provided support and advice. They also mediated conflicts between patients and caregivers and helped negotiate ground rules for relationships. In months 4 through 7, the tryout

9 Mary H. Larimer et al., "Healthcare and Public Service Use and Costs Before and After Provision for Housing for Chronically Homeless Persons with Severe Alcohol Problems," *JAMA* 301, no. 13 (April 2009): 1349, doi: 10.1001/jama.2009.414.

10 E. Susser et al., "Preventing Recurrent Homelessness among Mentally Ill Men: A 'Critical Time' Intervention after Discharge from a Shelter," *American Journal of Public Health* 87, no. 2 (1997): 256, https://doi.org/10.2105/ajph.87.2.256

phase, CTI workers observed the ground rules and made modifications if necessary. Months 8 and 9 were the termination phase, where meetings and parties were held to symbolize transfer of care.

The USO Group, during months 1 through 3, would get assistance from shelter staff upon request, and shelter staff would substitute for caregivers if necessary. In months 4 through 7, patients and caregivers could phone in for advice. Over an 18-month follow-up period, the average number of homeless nights was 30 for the CTI group and 91 for the USO group. The conclusion was that focusing on a critical time of transition might contribute to the prevention of recurrent homelessness of individuals with mental illness, even after the period of active intervention.

These studies appear to have contributed to the inspiration for the current Housing First models for the homeless. Housing First, when supported by HUD, provides more than just housing. This model, used by nonprofit agencies throughout America, also provides wraparound case management services to the tenants. Case management is intended to provide stability for homeless individuals, which increases their potential for success; it allows for accountability and promotes self-sufficiency. This housing, subsidized by the government, is supposed to be permanent and affordable; meaning that tenants pay a maximum of 30% of their income toward rent. Housing First, as managed by Pathways to Housing, targets individuals with disabilities,[11] and is supported through two HUD program models. They are the Supportive Housing model and the Shelter Plus Care model. The Pathways model has been recognized by the Substance Abuse and Mental Health Services Administration as an evidence-based practice. Models lay out a generic

---

11 Department of Housing and Urban Development, "Lead Technical Studies and Healthy Homes Technical Studies," Federal Register, vol. 72, no. 48, March 13, 2007.

program design, and programs operationalize these models to serve the actual clients.[12] These are some of the models that provided the early claims for the effectiveness of Housing First. Below is a history of the actions taken at the federal level that would eventually create a major shift in funding policy for homeless services across the United States.

In 2008, the US Congress appropriated $25 million in the McKinney–Vento Homeless Assistance Grants to show the effectiveness of rapid rehousing programs (e.g., Housing First). In February of 2009 President Obama signed the American Recovery and Reinvestment Act, part of which addressed homeless prevention by allocating $1.5 billion for rapid rehousing programs. In May of 2009, President Obama signed the Homeless Emergency Assistance and Rapid Transition to Housing (HEARTH) Act, reauthorizing HUD's homeless assistance programs. This act required HUD to create regulations implementing the new McKinney program.[13,14]

These acts reestablished the direction of homeless services across the United States for the next decade, making it extremely difficult to provide any homeless solutions that were not tied to permanent housing and Housing First principals if the program was going to rely on some form of federal and or state funds.

Not All that Glitters

What followed these case studies and the implementation of the HEARTH Act was a rush to rapid rehousing and other Housing

---

12 Monarch Housing Associates, "Pathways to Housing Evidence-Based Practice by HHS," March 30, 2008, https://monarchhousing.org2008/03/30/pathways-to-housing

13 National Alliance to End Homelessness, "Summary of HEARTH Act," October 21, 2008, http://endhomelessness.org/resource/summary-of-hearth-act-2/

14 National Alliance to End Homelessness, "Summary of HEARTH Act."

First models, and the rapid abandonment of virtually all homeless transitional housing models. It wasn't because everyone concluded that those programs no longer worked. It was because the funding stream for most of the country's local Continuum of Care programs relied heavily on the HUD funds allocated to their communities. One key component to catch here is that this move was never about better long-term solutions that would serve the interests of the homeless; it was about getting people off of the street and into housing. The following are a few of the critics.

Ralph DaCosta Nunez, the president and CEO of the Institute for Children, Poverty & Homelessness, who is also a professor at Columbia, predicted this one-size-fits-all is destined to fail, as statistics in New York City indicated.[15] Dr. Nunez described the approach as "public stupidity" rather than public policy. He complained that Housing First is all that is left after the other poverty programs have been underfunded or eliminated.

Sharam Kohan, a social policy expert and economist, compared the Housing First model to Panelák of the former communist countries that tried to end homelessness by providing permanent and unconditional public housing. Dr. Kohan criticized the Housing First model for following Panelák's failed philosophy and approaches. He pointed to a growing number of reports from communities that have implemented Housing First programs, saying that they have "created a new generation of slums and slumlords."[16]

---

15 Institute for Children, Poverty & Homelessness, "Rapidly Rehousing Homeless Families: New York City—A Case Study," *Reports* (April 1, 2013), https://www. icphusa.org/reports/rapidly-rehousing-homeless-families/

16 Sharam Kohan, "Housing First Lacks True Merit" Harvard Law School (blog), January 16, 2016. https://web.archive.org/web/20160424040539/http://blogs. harvard.edu/kohan/housing-first-lacks-true-merit/

Housing First has been criticized on its failure to address broader service outcomes, namely, substance abuse. The criticisms have been rebutted on the grounds that Housing First is a program model designed to end homelessness, not reduce substance abuse. This statement had to be made by an individual who never spent time researching the homeless population. Anyone who has worked for more than a few weeks with people who have experienced homelessness knows that one of the biggest factors preventing people from being able to maintain stable housing is substance abuse, which is directly linked to mental health problems. These two issues are virtually inseparable with most people who have lived on the street.

Dennis Watson and colleagues concluded: "In a rapid review and document analysis of Housing First scholarly literature in the US and Canada, it has been shown that these literatures are severely lacking in the implementation and explicit mention of Harm Reduction."[17]

Over the past decade there have been numerous articles supporting rapid rehousing and other Housing First models, citing data on improved outcomes for homeless individuals and cost reductions for providing services. Similarly, there have been numerous articles[18,19,20] critical of the one-size-fits-all application of Housing First.

---

17 Dennis Watson et al. "Housing First and Harm Reduction: A Rapid Review and Document Analysis of the US and Canadian Open-Access Literature," *Harm Reduction Journal* 14, no. 30 (2017), https://doi.org/10.1186/s12954-017-0158-x

18 Stephen Eide, "Housing First and Homelessness: The Rhetoric and the Reality," Manhattan Institute report (April 2020), https://media4.manhattan-institute.org/sites/default/files/housing-first-and-homelessness-SE.pdf.

19 Christopher Rufo, "The 'Housing First' Approach Has Failed: Time to Reform Federal Policy and Make it Work for Homeless Americans," The Heritage Foundation (August 2020), https://www.heritage.org/housing/report/the-housing-first-approach-has-failed-time-reform-federal-policy-and-make-it-work

20 Carlyn Zwarenstein, "Housing First and the Homeless Crisis: What Went Wrong?" FilterMag (July 2020), https://filtermag.org/housing-first-homelessness-crisis/

The disagreement among social service experts is not whether Housing First might work for a large group of homeless people; it is whether substantial groups of people who are currently homeless need to first address the issues that led them to homelessness. Many experts feel that those issues need to be addressed *prior to* moving into independent housing. They include things like substance abuse, co-occurring mental health issues, barriers to employment, and life skills training. There are many issues that will hinder someone who has been low-functioning for months or years, only surviving on the streets, from having the tools to manage a household and a lease and be comfortable in a community setting. In an article published by the Manhattan Institute titled "Housing First and Homelessness: The Rhetoric and the Reality,"[21] researchers made this distinction between service models: "Whereas Housing First providers hold themselves, most of all to the standard of residential stability—keeping the most clients housed for the longest periods—linear style programs often viewed residential stability as secondary to larger goals of independence or health." ("Linear style" refers to moving people through stages of care to eventually be ready for independent housing.)

The goal is to create a homeless service system where there is potential for individuals to leave generational poverty and transient living behind for good. It should be an effort to permanently reduce the homeless population one individual at a time. It is a matter of providing the time and the tools that are needed to overcome barriers and reach potential for those who choose to try. The questions of resources and costs always create topics of debate, especially when it comes to expending resources on "those people."

---

21 Eide, "Housing First and Homelessness."

The argument that it costs too much to invest in these other areas of intense homeless services really can't be substantiated. It has no credibility when these services are viewed as a short-term option. It has even less credibility when they are considered as a long-term investment. It is time to move on and share the experiences of the last 6 years, complete with the success, failures, and the actual costs of providing services that make a difference. Then we can start a discussion about finding better alternatives.

CHAPTER 7

The Roots of Disruptive Change

HUD Funds

One of the largest, if not the largest, funding sources for homeless services has been the federal Department of Housing and Urban Development (HUD). Sacramento County, through their contract agency Sacramento Steps Forward, was receiving $10.67 million per year from HUD in 2014–2017.[22] There is a collective submission process that is completed through a cooperative effort of the local Continuum of Care (COC) each year. It begins with HUD publishing their annual Notice of Funds Availability (NOFA). This funding is usually made available through HUD in June of each year, with the application package due in late August. The application package is made up of a collection of independent program components, which are operated by the local service providers. They are

---

22 Sacramento Steps Forward, *2017 Annual Report*, 2018, https://www.sacramen tostepsforward.org/wp-content/uploads/2018/07/2017-Annual-Report-FINAL-1. pdf.

responsible for preparing and submitting their part of the annual funding request. It is a fairly complex process that uses a point system to rank the individual programs. That process does not need to be detailed here.

A Conflict of Interest

It is important, however, to point out that the successes of getting programs funded are influenced by the recommendations of the local COC board each year. There were other influences that surfaced in 2015 in the Sacramento region. First, the county had contracted a new nonprofit agency to manage and monitor the use of HUD funds coming into Sacramento each year. That also put them in control of the annual NOFA application process. If the total award from HUD grew each year, so too did the operating budget of the monitoring agency. The agency CEO who was hired to oversee these tasks also became, by default, the chairman of the COC board. This appointment established a built-in conflict of interest about which programs and providers would be supported. The agency's budget would grow by supporting the programs that qualified for the most funding, whether or not they provided the most benefit to the population. This is exactly what happened in Sacramento and, I suspect, many other areas of the country. The additional fallout from this debacle was that funding for some programs that were providing great outcomes was prematurely discontinued to free-up those funds for a different use. Of course, the big losers were the potential homeless clients. New programs, designated for funding, were not ready to open or they were in experimental mode and couldn't provide the housing or services despite getting a lot of money to spend. Conversely, those programs that were continuing to provide housing and great services lost their funding.

Mather Community Campus had been a top-rated program in the Sacramento County NOFA for years. The ratings were based on the HUD point system; the point system awarded the programs that were producing the best outcomes with the lowest recidivism rate while matching the existing HUD criteria for preferred programming. Based on this analytical analysis, MCC was awarded the highest grant amount (up to $6 million by 2014) in our COC for many years. It is also noteworthy to point out that many of the other social service providers that were a part of the local COC relied on MCC as the place to refer the clients that they felt were capable of becoming self-sufficient. This created a very supportive atmosphere for MCC within the COC during the application process, at least for a while.

When HUD announced the pending move to the Housing First model (and the move away from transitional housing), there was some confusion about how the shift to that program model was going to unfold in our COC. There were also questions about how the new underlying guidelines were going to be implemented. One of the most onerous and disruptive requirements from HUD was the mandate to move to a regionwide process for identifying and serving the targeted population that was called **coordinated entry**. This mandate would end up comprising the most difficult, confusing, and disruptive initial changes to the existing system of care, so much so that there needs to be an attempt to explain the change and the early problems it caused before telling the rest of this story.

The Coordinated Entry Plan

The "plan" was not so much a plan as it was a process mandate from HUD to any community-wide homeless system of care that was going to continue to request HUD funding. At the time, HUD was funding approximately $1.5 billion per year, across the nation, for homeless services. There was nothing in place to supplant that much money for the homeless service models that had relied on HUD funding. As part of their new role of prioritizing housing solutions, HUD also added the coordinated entry requirement to create a new-client identification and distribution system. It was a system that was supposed to help facilitate their new goal of determining who would get the first available housing options.

Further complicating the issue were new definitions from HUD that would specify who would be considered "technically homeless," and therefore eligible for the HUD housing options. These new definition changes removed a segment of truly homeless people who had previously qualified for shelter or other related services. The lack of direction on how to replace an existing system of care that depended on direct referrals from the service providers with coordinated entry created chaos within the COC. The system design was going to attempt to create a program that would distribute clients from a centralized, internet-based system on a weekly timetable. HUD's redefining of who would be considered homeless only added to the confusion. The following were the stated requirements for coordinated entry:

- Register all homeless persons in your region in the Homeless Management Information System.

- Screen all of those individuals through a "Vulnerability Indexing" tool (self-assessment test).

- Based on the self-assessment, rank the population from the "most vulnerable" to "least vulnerable."

- Begin placing the population in the first available beds based on the most vulnerable being served first.

Registration into the system and vulnerability testing were to be done by a new group of social workers called "navigators." This is not a personal affront to those who became navigators, but the pay was barely above minimum wage and there was no substantive work history required. The navigators were tasked with going out into the community, including under the bridges, in and around abandoned buildings, along the river, behind commercial business centers, and anywhere else homeless were staying. They were supposed to locate, register, and provide the "test" to any homeless individuals they found. The vulnerability test was "self-scored" based on each individual's own assessment of their personal issues. It includes history related to their length of homelessness, alcohol and drug use, their physical and mental health condition, and their age, education, and work history. To their credit, many of the navigators learned on the job how to be effective at this work. However, being effective at finding, testing, and ranking the homeless population according to their "vulnerability" did not fit with the system of care that had been developed over decades that was based on totally different criteria.

Communities were allotted 2 years to get this system built, populated, and operational. This is another idea that when reviewed just on the potential merits of the four objectives would seem to have some strong appeal. The design and initial rollout of coordinated entry was compacted into a fairly short period. We had discussions with the designer in December of 2016 and were trying to integrate their system by the following April. All programs were impacted by the following existing complications:

- Coordinated entry was replacing a system of referrals that had been in place for over 50 years.

- Coordinated entry was only focused on the intakes of new clients. There was no consideration for homeless treatment programs that historically had moved clients to different service level options when they were ready.

- In our community, the organization responsible for implementing and managing the new system chose not to create a "pilot" program to work through any transition problems.

- Despite the fact that the entire COC had evolved organically around specific service models, coordinated entry was designed to place the most vulnerable individuals first in the first available bed, regardless of where it was located or the provider's historical service model. This created mismatches of individuals' needs to the services available.

- Individuals referred from the coordinated entry system could not be turned away for substance abuse issues, issues related to mental health, or their criminal backgrounds (except in a few rare instances).

A quick review of the referral system of care that was abruptly replaced will illustrate some of the problems with coordinated entry that led to complicating issues later. There was a brief summary earlier about the basics of the referral system that was in place for many years in social services, but it deserves a little further clarity.

Replacing the Referral System

Prior to coordinated entry, most services for the homeless began with placement or acceptance into shelters. Single and family shelters have offered a variety of services over the years, but they were almost exclusively intended to provide evening shelter, including a place to sleep, a meal, and a place to clean up, including taking a shower. A few offered 24-hour stays and links to other services. Homeless clients in need of higher levels of care such as substance abuse recovery or mental health services were usually referred to existing programs that were designed and available to best fit their needs. There were a few shelters during this period that offered the additional services of alcohol and drug recovery programs. There were also specific agencies that specialized in alcohol and drug rehabilitation programs. There were other social service programs that offered a higher level of care for people with more advanced mental health needs and/or physical disabilities. Finally, there were transitional housing programs for the homeless that offered temporary housing solutions, with programming designed to build a path to leave homelessness permanently. These programs included life-skill training, pre-employment and vocational training, and the opportunity to work through barriers to employment. There were also housing placement services.

The intended trajectory for the homeless on the street was to get them off the street and into a homeless shelter, where they could be stabilized and evaluated for additional care. Some of these individuals with less complicated barriers, after being stabilized short-term, could find work and move out on their own. Others with more complex needs might be considered for placement in a recovery program, a mental health program, or a transitional housing program, where multiple services were offered. Often an individual might pass through a shelter to a recovery program and then into transitional housing as an opportunity to leave homelessness. In actuality, all of this was occurring simultaneously, including "back referrals" if an individual working through an addiction relapsed. There was an effective and cooperative system to facilitate movement.

At Mather, a provider meeting would be held every 4 to 6 months to reestablish those relationships and have clarifying conversations about the other common issues involving homeless care. The process described was eliminated by coordinated entry and its implementation. It is hard to know how much the loss of this creativity, cooperation, and willingness to work toward common goals has cost our system of care. These exchanges were supplementing a process developed to work through the issues that had contributed to people being homeless. Housing First and coordinated entry bypassed these steps. The time spent sharing ideas has been replaced with trying to figure out how to navigate in the new era of coordinated entry, limited services, limited funding for services, and limited collaboration. These changes created a void for many providers who had relied on sending their clients to Mather and had no other alternative when that option was removed.

Coordinated entry was a federal idea. It was based on policy-makers' assumption that in every city the most vulnerable were not getting fair treatment. There was a belief that all providers were se-lecting the clients who were the easiest to serve and would produce the best outcomes. This in turn left the most difficult cases without services, and they believed this was fueling the growth of homeless-ness. Based on those assumptions, the policy-makers in our federal government paved the way for Housing First programs to domi-nate the availability of federal funds for homeless housing programs. Coinciding with Housing First, HUD introduced the mandate to develop a coordinated entry system and redefined who was to be considered homeless, which completely ignored approximately 50 years of carefully constructed local homeless services in many local Continuums of Care. Not only has this process continued to fail, it began by interrupting the ongoing care of thousands of homeless people and placed thousands more in new, unproven programs that also failed.

To date, HUD has continued to push their agenda without any real attempt to take a critical look at the results. They continue to use selective data when reporting results. It is the mechanism to keep the funding flowing into these communities. Locally, these programs are now being buoyed by a new group of providers who look to keep tight control on the new money they have found for their program. Meanwhile, the number of people in our homeless population continues to grow and grow, and the underlying social issues that threaten the fabric of our communities are getting worse and worse.

We have now presented a history lesson of the events that most impacted homeless services over the past 10 to 15 years. The sole reliance on Housing First has caused funding limitations that continue to reduce opportunity for those who are homeless. Issues triggered by these limitations include the design and rollout errors of coordinated entry. These errors have been compounded by the complete move away from programs that offered critical services for assisting the homeless, such as Mather Community Campus. The new definition of who can be considered homeless is another flawed attempt at artificially underreporting the population and preventing thousands in need from being eligible for services.

CHAPTER 8

Comparing the New Service Models with What Was Replaced

THERE IS A LOT TO COVER IN THIS CHAPTER. ULTIMATELY, we will provide a comparison of the services that were available to homeless clients at the Mather transitional housing program (now closed), with the Housing First programs that are intended to provide housing and service alternatives to the homeless (operating today). To put these comparisons in context, it is important to understand the unique circumstances that create the affordable housing shortages in California. It is also important to have a closer look at the issues (barriers) that the homeless population has to address to consider any form of independent living.

We will start by looking at the other impacts to service delivery that came in the form of policy and procedural changes from HUD at the same time. These policy changes were requirements that local COCs had to adopt to have access to HUD funds. They included changes in the definitions of who was considered technically homeless and therefore eligible for services. Additionally, the use of HUD funds in homeless service would no longer allow service providers to refuse services or housing to individuals who were actively using alcohol or drugs. Last, they included a mandate, defined in the previous chapter, that required each COC to create and operationalize a homeless population tracking and client delivery system called coordinated entry. Funds for homeless service that originated at the state level also adopted these policy changes.

When reviewing these issues collectively, it is important to remember that there was a wait-list for Mather of more than 200 people that was wiped out in 1 day by the mandated switch to coordinated entry. It was devastating to the people waiting to get in, and to the service providers and families who were counting on their clients and family members getting into the program. There were another 100 clients in the middle of their program at Mather who later lost all of their service options when the program was closed. Remember this point when we get to the review of services that were available to these people at Mather prior to its closing. These 300-plus people were among the many (easily thousands nationally) we referred to earlier whose service programs were abandoned when HUD eliminated funding transitional housing programs. In this chapter, we will look at some of the striking differences in the program make-up, operational intent, and services available. But let's start by reviewing the impact that the HUD policy changes would have on homeless services.

HUD's Definition of Homeless and the Move Away from Transitional Housing

In the last chapter, we noted that HUD issued changes to the definition of who was technically homeless. One major target of those changes was aimed at eliminating the transitional housing option as a continuing eligible service model for the homeless. HUD published a 102-page document[23] in November of 2011 that included public comment on their proposed "final rule" to define who was homeless. It included questions that were submitted from the impacted "public." On page 5 of that document, the report starts to highlight the changes. The very first change listed is the definition of what qualifies as a homeless shelter, with the acknowledgment that people staying in shelters are considered homeless. It further states: "Shelter includes 'Emergency Shelter' but not 'Transitional Housing.'" The public comment on page 21 suggested that a clearer standard was needed for the term *shelter*.

The public comments also included one that suggested transitional housing needed to remain included because of restrictions on shelters in certain geographic areas. HUD disagreed that transitional housing should be included in the definition of shelter for persons who are exiting institutions "but who have resided in such institutions for more than 90 days." A few pages later it adds this clarification: "If an individual had spent more than 90 days receiving services in a publicly funded program they were considered 'institutionalized' and not homeless regardless of their situation prior to getting services or their lack of permanent housing solutions upon release." This additional clarification meant homeless being served in transitional housing no longer qualified for any continuing homeless service. To be precise, transitional housing clients could not take advantage of rapid rehousing programs, publicly funded recovery programs, or any other homeless services after 90 days in a transitional housing program. The 100 pages of comments, questions, and answers discussed in the proposed "final rule"

---

23 Department of Housing and Urban Development, "Homeless Emergency Assistance and Rapid Transition to Housing: Defining 'Homeless,'" 24 CFR Parts 91, 576, 582, and 583 [Docket No. FR-5333-F-02] RIN 2506-AC26].

left many questions unanswered, including what was the definition of an institution. Rather than establishing a fixed list of qualifying institutions, HUD wrote that they would provide guidance in the future. In practice, it looked like anyone who had resided for more than 90 days in any program or interim-housing solution was no longer considered homeless.

There were also unanswered questions about whether a person or family is considered to have adequate nighttime residence (therefore not qualifying as homeless). The question was, "If there were multiple people sleeping in a building that was 'originally designed to be a residence' but was dilapidated, with or without water or electricity, would they be considered homeless?" HUD's answer was: "HUD recognizes that vulnerable populations that live in overcrowded housing (with or without electricity or water) are excluded from the definition of homeless; however, the language 'place designed for or ordinarily used as a regular sleeping accommodation' is statutory."[24] This response feels like an excuse not to accept responsibility to provide basic human services.

To make it harder to qualify for access to funding, adequate records must be kept to verify that an individual or family is in fact literally homeless according to their final rule. This can sometimes be difficult and is almost always tedious. The penalty for not having adequate documentation is the requirement for the organization providing service to pay back the funds to the monitoring agency. Depending on the relationship with the monitoring agency and how they view the service provider, that can be a delicate and potentially costly issue. HUD added a catchall category for qualifying additional people for services—the "imminently homeless"

---

24 Department of Housing and Urban Development, "Homeless Emergency Assistance and Rapid Transition to Housing: Defining 'Homeless.'"

category. This is someone whose current circumstances are likely to lead them to homelessness. These situations also require supporting documentation that, if not deemed adequate, can force a service provider to have to repay the funds received for those services. This is a very slippery slope that often keeps providers from taking the risks needed to service some homeless in these questionable categories.

These definition changes were put in place to prioritize who should be eligible for public funds when it came to social service programming. It isn't exactly clear what all the definition nuances were intended to do other than eliminate transitional housing programs and reduce the number of people who could be counted as homeless. Despite the changes in the definitions of who was considered homeless, the homeless population throughout California, including in Sacramento, is growing every year. Over the past 2 years, the publicly advanced solutions to accommodate this growing problem have been primarily focused on addressing a housing shortage. This is the result of the new federal and state funding for homeless programs, which now requires the inclusion of additional affordable housing units for qualifying programs. At the same time, the discussions for developing expanded supportive services for homeless people have only been philosophical to this point and fall dramatically short of providing people the tools needed to find a path to independence.

Recognizing the Impact of Alcohol and Drug Addictions

Meanwhile, there is a lack of discussion or debate over alcohol and drug addictions being significant factors leading to and sustaining homelessness. The Housing First advocates just remind us that their primary objective is to provide housing solutions, not substance abuse solutions. It is difficult to know whether there is a deliberate denial of any connection between the two or just an unwillingness to include this issue as part of the homeless crisis. We submit that anyone who has worked with the homeless population knows that if the addictions are not addressed and recovery programming is not put in place, there is zero opportunity to make meaningful progress on slowing the growth of homelessness.

According to HUD spokesman Brian E. Sullivan, as quoted in a February 2018 article in *The Morning Call*, HUD's goal was to make homelessness "'rare, brief and nonrecurring.' … Under the old model, it met none of the objectives, he said. 'We were managing homelessness, not ending it.'"[25] It looks like the new model is not meeting those objectives either. In addition to that fact, we may now also have to accept the realities that the related problems of crime, mental health, and public hygiene that are directly linked to addiction will continue to have a place to grow among the homeless. Who is going to manage those issues going forward? Now that we have identified who is being served and who and what are being excluded, we can look at the system that was mandated by HUD to organize and deliver the services to the population they defined as homeless.

Coordinated Entry Was Doomed to Fail

As outlined in the last chapter, the goal of coordinated entry was to create a master list of homeless people and, through a self-scored evaluation tool, rank the population according to their vulnerability. The most vulnerable would receive available services first. Tracking down people who are homeless and providing an evaluation of

---

25 Tim Darragh, "How a HUD policy change is upending housing for the homeless," *The Morning Call*, February 5, 2018.

their current condition is a worthwhile endeavor. Also creating an internet-based tracking system for the population and their system of care has real value. These are the two most fundamental pieces of the coordinated entry system.

Placing people in HUD-funded programs through coordinated entry prohibits denying entry to individuals who are currently using alcohol and/or drugs. The system falls short by not triaging people prior to placement; it ignores any opportunity to consider the best service options for an individual prior to placing them in the system. This was a particular stumbling block in Northern California. We have already established that the local COC had self-organized their service delivery system around the specific needs of the individuals. The system had been developed over decades and functioned extremely well based on a system of cooperative planning. Homeless people would generally take their first step off the streets by entering a shelter. Then there would be the additional placement options to consider, as explained in chapter 6, which provided a progression of treatment options that targeted the eventual goal of removing individuals from homelessness for good through employment to permanent housing.

With the rollout of coordinated entry, there was nothing put in place to utilize the existing COC structure and ongoing programming. The referral system of care moving people through stages simply stopped. The most vulnerable clients would be assigned the first beds available regardless of the provider's previous service model. Even more problematic, when this system was coupled with the new Housing First options, it was doomed to fail. Here is a simple example. Coordinated entry became the required system used to place homeless into the publicly funded (HUD) programs. This included the new rapid rehousing programs. Typically, these programs will pay 3 to 6 months of rent, along with other deposit requirements necessary for the individual to get market-rate housing (generally rentals). When the subsidy runs out, the client only has to pay a maximum of 30% of their income for rent going forward. The client will also get "light touch" case management services for up to 6 months. Coordinated entry is strictly tasked with serving the most vulnerable people first. Almost exclusively, these were the clients with the highest level of needs or those who were the lowest functioning at the time they were tested. Unfortunately, this made them the least likely to be able to live independently and made them the worst fit for rapid rehousing. So, the better the navigators did their job of serving the most vulnerable first, the worse the outcomes were in these programs.

It wasn't just rapid rehousing programs that struggled. The impact on the Mather program was particularly harsh. After the immediate elimination of the two-hundred-person waiting list, the agency managing coordinated entry began to send the most vulnerable from the local homeless population to Mather. Instead of serving the people who had been on a waiting list and who wanted the chance to turn their lives around, the program saw fifteen to twenty people per week who had never heard of the program and were the least likely to succeed. Intake procedure at Mather for 20 years had included alcohol and drug testing to screen applicants. Mather staff had also conducted random drug tests during the clients' residency in an attempt to maintain a clean and sober community. The program was directed to cease all testing prior to and after move-in. This is a snapshot of the current homeless system for managing placements and services in Northern California and in most other major metropolitan areas. Each area has its unique set of circumstances that have to be dealt with to make coordinated entry function.

California's Housing Challenges

California is unique in the fact that it is home to 27% of the national homeless population.[26] It is also home to some of the most expensive real estate in the nation, and it may be the most difficult and costly state in the US to do new developments of any kind. Like most metropolitan areas, our area in Northern California is heavily dependent on HUD for funding homeless services. That was before the COVID-19 pandemic hit in early 2020.

The California state budget, at this writing, is projected to have a more than $50 billion budget shortfall for 2020, and major cuts to social services have already begun. With millions of people currently out of work and many small businesses on the brink of elimination, the problem of homelessness is only going to grow. Throw in the reductions to sentencing requirements and the accelerated release of prisoners in California and we are looking at a potential social disaster sooner rather than later.

But let's pause here and look at some of the new housing ideas that have been generated to deal with the growing population of homeless in Sacramento, from local government leaders prior to the pandemic.

- Erect tent cities in metropolitan areas. Discuss moving their location periodically.

- Stack storage containers and convert them into places people can sleep.

- Build more low-income housing units across the state.

---

26 Homelessness Policy Research Institute, "State of Homelessness in California Fact Sheet," 2020, https://socialinnovation.usc.edu/wp-content/uploads/2020/02/Homelessness-in-CA-Fact-Sheet-v3.pdf.

- Construct tiny homes (400 to 500 sq. ft.) without kitchens or baths and place them on existing residential grounds or church properties and share existing kitchens and bathrooms.

- Create safe campgrounds.

- Convert hotel rooms into shelter spaces.

- Build more shelters in every community.

These ideas are in addition to the continued growth of rapid rehousing and other Housing First solutions. Let's discuss these options a little further. The primary difficulty with tent cities and/ or stacked storage containers is finding locations that first, will be publicly approved and second, can provide the basic sanitary services required to keep the surrounding area from becoming a public health hazard. The idea to move them periodically is only to placate the local citizens who would be impacted. Moving these programs adds enormous logistic and infrastructure expense issues and further complicates the problems of providing adequate sanitation.

Certainly, building more low-income housing has a lot of merit if you can mitigate some of the major development problems. One of the biggest hurdles in the State of California is the enormous weight of the "soft costs" (environmental impact reports, engineering, architecture, permits, etc.) involved in residential development. As a result of Proposition 13, there are not enough funds available in every community for the improvements needed to support new residential construction. California Proposition 13, which passed in 1978, reduced current property taxes on homes, businesses, and farms by 57%, and created a cap on future increases in property tax at a maximum of 2% per year, after the initial valuation.[27] This has resulted in a lack of state revenue increases to support future infrastructure improvements. Without the needed resources, the state and local cities have pushed those costs on to developers. Those costs are on top of obtaining the property and include preparing environmental impact reports (and defending the legal challenges that come with every environmental filing), processing zoning changes, navigating the public approval process, connecting adequate infrastructure, and then doing the actual physical development of the location prior to obtaining building permits. Building permits these days are loaded with so many local fees it is staggering. The fact that it takes years to get all the public approvals prior to starting construction is another huge factor, and coupled with all of the other cost factors, "affordable housing" becomes an unrealistic objective. Also, there is always neighborhood resistance to affordable housing ("not in my backyard"). Regardless of all of those roadblocks, affordable housing has to remain some part of the solution in California. Revealing the magnitude of this problem, there was a report published in 2019 by the California Housing Partnership titled "California's Housing Emergency Update."[28] The report cited that California needs 1.4 million more affordable housing units. It also cited a 23% decline in low-income tax credits. The proposed solutions

---

27 California Tax Data, "What Is Proposition 13?," http://www.californiataxdata.com/pdf/Prop13.pdf.

28 California Housing Partnership, "California's Housing Emergency Update," 2019, https://1p08d91kd0c03rlxhmhtydpr-wpengine.netdna-ssl.com/wp-content/uploads/2019/03/CHPC_HousingNeedReport_2019_PRINT_High-Res1.pdf.

in the report are intriguing, but they would take years to produce enough revenue to have a significant impact.

Converting hotels to shelter beds and building more shelter space can be another important consideration, providing we reinstate some options to move some of this population out of homelessness for good and find other places to move those who need more help into a variety of permanent housing solutions. Congregating people in shelters for long periods of time produces very little movement forward and should only be used for short-term planning.

Permanent Supportive Housing

The current homeless system of care appears to define success as moving an individual from the street to a permanent supportive housing (PSH) option. This means that the individual will receive government support for their housing needs indefinitely. Because there is such a shortage of affordable housing for this use, priority should be given to individuals who cannot earn enough income or receive enough income from disability benefits to pay their housing costs. Others who are not thought to need PSH will be placed in the rapid rehousing projects with the intention of providing some of the financial resources to obtain their housing. The failure rate in some of these programs has been staggering, and the process is giving birth to more slums. During the COVID-19 pandemic, landlords have not been able to evict clients for non-payment, which is masking a larger problem and adding another social stress point.

Every community needs PSH options for a part of the homeless population. Also, individuals who have been properly triaged and supported can be very successful within the rapid rehousing programs. We have created a growing problem because the system has failed for the last 3 years to identify the people who might make a good fit for rapid rehousing. Also lacking has been the adequate services needed to provide the tools and support for them to remain independent. Now, because so many have not received the services needed to become independent, there is a growing reliance on finding affordable PSH options going forward. These housing options are already becoming harder and harder to find an issue that will continue to get worse in the near future.

Transitional Housing Services (the Mather Example)

The important point to make is that the goal of the transitional housing model was to help those who were homeless move into a position of self-sufficiency by the time they were exited from the program. Self-sufficiency is defined as having a job that provides enough income, or adequate disability benefits, along with enough savings for the necessary deposits, to move into and support a market-rate housing option. This is what transitional housing was designed to accomplish. For the population who was coming into the Mather program, that required a lot of work. I hope to start a discussion on the possibility of bringing these kinds of programs back in the next best form and function. It could be a transitional housing program or something unique that offers similar opportunities.

Homeless Barriers to Independent Living

It is important to understand the issues facing the homeless person who has been living on the streets for an extended period. They include an unavoidable slow diminishing of the basic tools needed to live independently. What also happens over time is that an individual accumulates barriers to employment and housing that greatly reduce their options. Below is a list of the "barrier profiles" of clients who entered the Mather program in 2016 (these percentages remained virtually unchanged for 15 years). We believe these numbers are representative of anyone's profile who has spent much time living on the street and chronically homeless.[29]

- 80% were dealing with substance abuse issues (addictions).

- 99% did not have an active bank account (most for at least 2 years).

- 100% had no savings or owned any assets.

- 70% had criminal records (usually 30% to 40% were on parole or probation).

- 90% did not have an active drivers' license.

- 75% had not finished high school or obtained a GED.

- Very few had any recent employment (the last 3 to 5 years) to list on a resume.

- 100% had no credit or bad credit.

---

[29] Statistics are from internal Volunteers of America client barrier profile records at Mather, from 2015 to 2018.

- 1 out of 100 had a car. Value had to be less than $2,000 to qualify for public services.

- Past housing experiences were either minimal or included an eviction.

- Very few had any relevant vocational training.

Virtually all government-funded social services programs are now providing Housing First benefits to people regardless of whether or not they remain sober. To demonstrate the impact of this important restriction, we can look back at a time at Mather when our local county prohibited our enforcement of sobriety. Over a 14-month period, the program results deteriorated dramatically in the number of people getting jobs and moving into their own housing. There was also a significant increase in drug-related crime and a decline in the safety of living in the community.

Those who understand drug and alcohol addiction know that until these issues are mitigated, there is little chance for a person who has been homeless to achieve sustainable independent living. Regardless, the new policy guidelines from the federal, state, and local governments intentionally removed sobriety as a requirement for homeless individuals to get funds for housing options. One could speculate that part of the overall federal policy decision process determined that alcohol and drug rehabilitation of the homeless was costing too much. The alternate plan becomes sheltering them in locations that are the least disruptive in the community (i.e., slums, tent cities, storage containers, converted hotels, etc.) and hoping the individuals will seek treatment on their own. The problem is that we know that trying to defeat an addiction without professional help is like asking someone to develop their own cancer cure. What will it take to have policy-makers realize we are dealing with a pervasive disease?

Everything else on the list presented above became a barrier to getting employment and sustaining housing. All of the barriers have to be removed to provide people a chance to become self-sufficient. Certain political groups and government agencies insist that every human being has a right to housing. I would argue that mitigating the issues on this list should be considered a right of every human being. You just can't buy into the belief that all people struggling with these issues got there making bad choices. That is a very bad argument that breaks down quickly when you know their stories, and the stories that are presented in this book show *why* it is a bad argument. There are hundreds of circumstances and conditions in people's lives that can result in their becoming homeless. We met very few, over the years, who said that they made choices they knew would lead to their becoming homeless. How to take care of any one of these issues, let alone two, three, or four is a difficult question when you're living on the street. The Mather transitional housing program was all about providing the tools needed to live independently. All these services were part of a structured program that was available by *walking across the campus*, taking classes, or working with a specialist on removing barriers.

Differences between Transitional Housing and Rapid Rehousing

It is revealing to examine the major differences between services offered with transitional housing and those of rapid rehousing. Let's look at some direct comparisons.

94

Table 1. Comparison of services offered by two housing models.

Service provided	Transitional model	Rapid rehousing model
Housing	12 months rent-free	3–6 months subsidized rent
Case management	On-site	Off-site, periodic visits
24-hour support staff	Included	
Interest assessment	Included	
Individual service plan	Included	Included
Individual employment plan	Included	
Job coach	On-site	
Credit repair specialist	On-site	
Recovery meetings	On-site	Referrals available
Life skills training	On-site	
Meals	On-site	
Financial training	On-site	
Pre-employment training	On-site	
Clothes closet	On-site	Off-site
Vocational training	On-site	
Criminal record reduction	On-site	
Job fairs	On-site	
Hiring events	On-site	
Job retention	Included	
Housing specialist	On-site	Included
Licensed clinical social worker	On-site	

Housing First rapid rehousing programs provide wraparound case management services designed to provide stability for the homeless individuals. These wraparound services generally consist of the following, which are in addition to the 3 to 6 months of rent and the deposit subsidies:

- Three to six months of case management (1 to 2 times per week during this period);

- Help with learning how to maintain a clean home;

- Some assistance with the application for and follow-up on disability benefits;

- Some assistance with personal hygiene;

- Referrals to assistance with substance abuse;

- Referrals to county mental health services;

- Monitoring of guest activity.

Compared to the services that were available to students/clients at the Mather transitional housing program, there is a significant gap in the services provided now—services that are critical to getting an individual who has been chronically homeless ready to live independently. A Housing First case manager whom I interviewed said, "It feels like we are doing more harm than good by placing people in housing before they are ready." Approximately 50% of these clients have disability benefits, so there is some income to fall back on when the subsidy runs out. If those individuals are dealing with alcohol or drug addiction, it is just a matter of time until those needs outweigh the need to pay rent. The other 50% have to get some kind of employment to sustain their new housing. Without any of the pre-employment training, vocational training, or business relationships, it is very difficult for this group of people to find a job that pays a livable wage.

We have provided the origins for the Housing First models and a description of the programs and services that have been put in place the last 5 years. In our community, we do not have long-term data yet to fairly evaluate the outcomes. But we have seen an alarmingly high rate of failure in the first few years in these programs, as well as some serious issues in some of the neighborhoods where the population is concentrated, namely drug-related problems, including gang activity.

Chasing Federal Funds

The system of care that has now been adopted in virtually every US city followed the HUD money first (out of financial necessity), not a strategic plan. If you still don't believe that is the case, consider the statistics that reflect the make-up of the National HUD Homeless Assistance Grant Program over the past 14 years. In 2005, transitional housing programs were funded at $417,439,417; or 35% of the total national grant program. That same year PSH was awarded $595,483,232; or 50% of the total. In 2018, transitional housing was only awarded $66,342,036; or 3% of the national grant program. That same year PSH received $1,542,451,024; or 71% of the total.[30] This is the best evidence I can find to verify how bad federal policy, backed by huge dollars, can result in bad decisions locally, regardless of intent. The trend for reducing transitional housing funds would continue

---

30 Stephen Eide, "Housing First and Homelessness: The Rhetoric and the Reality," Manhattan Institute report (April 2020), https://media4.manhattan-institute.org/sites/default/files/housing-first-and-homelessness-SE.pdf.

into 2019, so it is no wonder that Mather would not survive. I am not convinced that this was because there were not enough funds available from other sources to cover the operating costs. It is more likely that our local policy-makers took the bait that it was time to give up on transitional housing.

As a side note, there is no evidence that a comprehensive financial analysis had been done in our region to evaluate the spending of taxpayers' money on county services for homeless care. Shouldn't we look more closely at what makes up the $100,000+ that is reportedly being spent on each homeless person per year living on the street in our communities? These are funds that are being spent with virtually no accountability regarding homeless services. The fact that hundreds of homeless people in our community are not getting adequate public services and are often subject to abuse by this system goes by virtually unnoticed.

The Defining Work of Mather

The solutions we are advocating require more work and more collaborative resources but come with a built-in guarantee for a more positive financial and social impact in our communities. The current system of care discounts dignity and respect as desired outcomes for the clients it is attempting to serve. This is unfortunate because we had a system where every client had a chance to reach their highest potential along with the dignity and respect that come through the effort and accomplishments of their work.

The defining work that was accomplished for Mather clients who completed the program was helping them build a foundation that could support independent living. For some, it was recovering what had been lost. For others, it was acquiring some needed skills and resources for the first time. It came in the form of barrier reduction, job training, substance abuse control, credit repair, budgeting, driver's licenses being reinstated, and learning how to contribute in a community setting prior to moving into independent housing. Along with vocational training, the final piece was gaining meaningful employment. The program elements were tied to a resident's housing status; if a student chose not to participate in the program elements, they could lose their housing. On the occasions when students were faced with losing their place at Mather, it wasn't necessarily the loss of housing that concerned them. Instead, the thought they most often expressed was that they might not get another opportunity to exit homelessness through this type of program. This concern led many to change their behavioral patterns so that they could stay.

Required program elements are no longer in fashion in the social services fields. Trauma-informed care is an important new parameter of care in dealing with people who have been traumatized. Policy-makers in favor of trauma-informed care have advocated dropping the "required" conditions in housing programs, citing the possibility of retraumatizing individuals. It is a fact that anyone who has spent significant time living on the street has experienced some form of trauma. I have studied trauma and moral injury for almost 4 years now and have added the topic of moral resiliency to my research. For people to experience a healthy emotional existence, a basic requirement is to be a vital and engaged part of a community. We are not wired to live alone or spend a lot of time in isolation. In order to meet that objective, we have to develop internal guidelines for mutual respect and consideration (personal integrity and relational integrity). It is almost impossible to create a culture that promotes these values without guidelines and structure. These guidelines and structure exist in all other segments of our daily lives, and they are also needed in homeless care in order to facilitate reintegration back into the community. I found that when people experienced the satisfaction and joy of helping another person accomplish something, it filled a need in their psyche that supports emotional health.

We need to continue to include elements of community building into programs designed to rehabilitate people who have experienced trauma and/or emotional damage. Mather Community Campus was already more than a place for homeless people to work on barrier reduction. It was a place where people *were cared for in a way that most of them had never experienced before.* I consider the closing of the Mather employment to housing program a tragic loss. There is literally no other place in our community today where single adults who are working to get out of homelessness can get housing with comprehensive services. It almost seems incomprehensible that we have gotten to this point.

It is time to introduce you to some of the staff who worked at the campus over the last 15 years and to share their stories of some of the experiences and people who influenced them while at Mather. The work that these people put in every day for years was stressful and at times extremely difficult. To a person, they loved their work and the program they served. What they accomplished over the years was remarkable. I will share some of our client stories, published with permission. I also have the stories from a few of the staff, who were former students at Mather. Hopefully, you will get a much better feel for the work done there through these true accounts of the people who worked there and/or went through the program.

CHAPTER 9

Key Mather Staff

Meet Greg Williams (Mather Staff)

Greg Williams held the title of support staff supervisor for the entire 6 years I was responsible for the Mather program, and had been in that position for several years before I got there. While support staff supervisor was his official title, unofficially everyone referred to Greg as the mayor of Mather. Greg has an uncanny memory for names and faces and there are very few students, if any, who came through Mather whom he wouldn't be able to name if he saw them or their picture, or even if he heard a description of them and when they were on the campus. Greg is 6'3" and weighs in the 250-pound range. He came equipped with a booming voice that easily commands attention. Nobody loved their job more than Greg did when our campus was full of singles and families. Greg, like many who end up caring for the people who are struggling to stay alive and relevant, didn't come floating in with a perfect background. Let's start with a summary look at Greg's history prior to coming to Mather.

Greg grew up in Modesto. He had a great childhood with both his mother and father. As he puts it, "I grew up in a strong Christian home with great parents." He has a brother and sister. His parents still live in the same home today. Greg was a straight-A student in his first 2 years in high school. The family went to church every Sunday and Greg attended bible study every Wednesday night. He was an overachiever and star on the high school baseball team, playing as a starter when he was a sophomore. Things changed dramatically between his sophomore and junior year in high school, when he discovered drugs and alcohol. Before Greg's junior year ended, he had joined the United States Air Force where he would spend the next 4 years. By the time he was discharged (honorably), he was, by his own admission, a full-blown alcoholic and using a variety of other recreational drugs. After leaving the Air Force, Greg went to work in the tire business at a company his father owned. When he was twenty-five, he was sure he was the heir to the family business. But his father ended up selling the business and working for the new owner. Greg followed him and continued to work in the tire business for a while. With help from his uncle, Greg managed to get his union card and secured a great paying job for a major construction company. He now had all the money he needed to support his drug and alcohol habits. With the support of his parents, these issues led him to enter his first alcohol and drug rehabilitation program when he was 27 years old.

He chose not to follow the Alcoholics Anonymous (AA) twelve-step program. He lasted 108 days clean and sober and then relapsed. He went back to his job with the construction company. At age 29, he got clean and sober again and entered his second rehabilitation program. He still chose not to follow the AA step program and this time lasted 9 months. The construction company let him come back again where he worked on and off for the next 2 years.

In 1994, Greg got sober for the third time, entered another program, and started actually doing some of the twelve-step work. He managed to stay sober for 2½ years. This time when he relapsed, he lost everything he had in 6 weeks. He lost his job, his girlfriend, his place to live, and his relationship with his parents. On October 27, 1996, he got clean and sober for the final time and entered a 90-day rehabilitation program.

As he was preparing to leave and go back to Modesto to pick up his old life, his counselor asked him: "Why would you do that? You don't have a job, you don't have a girlfriend or a place to live, and your 'old life' has not produced good results." He told Greg's dad to take him to Fair Oaks and put him in a long-term rehabilitation program where he could start over. So that is exactly what they did. Greg entered a transitional living rehabilitation program, which he completed. His dad helped him buy a house and supported him for the next 2 years. After 2 years, his dad asked him if he was ready to work again. He answered yes dad, I want to come to work for you. So, his dad hired him back as a warehouse manager, which he did for the next 3½ years. He ended up tearing a disk in his back and had to give up the warehouse job because of the physical demands. He was taking some classes at American River College at the time and met an individual who was working for Volunteers of America who introduced Greg to their human resource manager. The short story is Greg ended up taking a minimum wage job as a support staff monitor at Mather Community Campus. He was 7 years sober when he got hired.

Greg is still working at Mather Campus. He vowed to learn everything he could about the campus, the operations, the clients, the right way to provide a safe environment for the staff, and the diverse and complicated single and family clients who came there to turn their life around. It was inevitable that Greg would end up in charge of the twenty-one people who made up the support staff. Those who worked in support staff had jobs that were more complicated than I can explain. Support staff don't just keep the campus safe; they are a critical liaison between the rest of the staff and the clients. They are also a trusted person for a client to talk to at any hour of the day if needed. They worked with parole officers and probation officers whenever needed. They called the police and the ambulance services when needed. They wrote incident reports any time there was a client violation or a police officer or an ambulance on campus. They would do periodic safety checks when people were struggling or sick. They did weekly room inspections of every room on the campus. They were responsible for taking the drug testing samples and maintaining records of all of this activity. They brought clients their meals if they could not get to the dining hall for some reason. These tasks were carried out 24 hours a day, 7 days a week. They provide transportation services every day of the week for someone. They have even saved lives on several occasions under very stressful circumstances.

Today Greg has 24 years of sobriety. He has personally seen, assisted, motivated, and helped manage several thousand people who worked their way through this program and eventually found work and a permanent place to live. Chris Mann taught the first class he sat in on at Mather. Greg already knew Chris from other AA meetings. Greg told me, "I knew I was home from that moment on."

Greg immersed himself in the success of the program and the welfare of students who were living there. In addition to supervising the support staff, he taught classes, ate lunch with the students, and talked about his sobriety and how that saved his life. Ten years into the program, Beth Valentine became the program director. She started a new program component called Monday Morning Launch. The entire campus population was required to get up on

Monday morning, dress like they were going to work, and gather for a "kick-off" meeting. At that meeting there would be celebrations for every kind of success you could think of, from sobriety dates, to people getting jobs, reuniting with a family member, or completing a program element. Greg also took ownership of that meeting while I was director. Greg is very proud of the fact that he has attended seventeen graduations at Mather and had people come up and shake his hand and thank him for saving their son or daughter or brother or sister. He will tell you that the reason he is here doing what he is doing is because someone once reached out a hand to him, which started his recovery and eventually gave him his life back. No community has ever had a better, more dedicated mayor. He was here for about 5 years when another very important figure, Mariann Friedrich, arrived to manage the DHA office and brought a whole new energy to the campus.

Meet Mariann Friedrich
(Sacramento Department of Human Assistance)

There are some people who just seem born to invest their time and energy into improving the lives of others. You see it in teachers who are truly dedicated to their mission and in a handful of medical workers. Special individuals working in those fields tend to draw recognition from their community. This does not happen often with people working in the field of homeless services. Mariann Friedrich was put on the planet to serve people in need. Prior to coming to the Mather Campus, she worked with Child Protective Services (CPS). She arrived at Mather in 2005. While working with CPS, Mariann was attending church at the Newman Center. Once a month she and others from the church would go to Loaves and Fishes to help serve the homeless meals. "I absolutely loved the people I was serving," she said. She began to wonder how she could find a way to work with them full-time.

Based on her situation at the time, the options were limited. One day she got a call from a friend who told her there was a position open at Mather that would be perfect for her. She didn't really know anything about Mather except for the hate mail people had sent in about having homeless services at that location. She interviewed for the position and was hired. When Mariann started at CPS, she received very little training: "There's your desk, there's your caseload of twenty-seven people, see you later." She shadowed another person for 1 week and then was on her own. When she got to Mather, she was ready to hit the ground running. Her new supervisor told her to relax, "take a couple of weeks, walk around, meet the people, and get to know the program." That's exactly what she did, thinking, "This is not how you run a business." But she quickly realized that Mather was completely different from CPS. At CPS she was instructed not to get too personal with clients, to limit emotions and keep clear boundaries; it was strictly business. At Mather she found that clients were hugging her and telling her their life stories. Her first reaction was that the people had no boundaries and she was going to have to fix that problem. That didn't last very long, because she saw how much fun it could be and how much the staff at Mather loved what they were doing.

For Mariann, the process of interviewing prospective students and hearing their stories, and then seeing their reaction when they were accepted into the program, was a fabulous experience. One of the first major responsibilities Mariann took on was organizing the graduation, which took place in June. She knew nothing about graduations, but the process of being "thrown into the fire" ended up being the right move to get her fully immersed in the campus. That year Maria Shriver, Governor Schwarzenegger's wife, showed up and donated office supplies, school supplies for the children, backpacks, and more. As she handled that, she realized that her new job was to do anything that the team needed her to do, and that's what she did. When she was bored, she would wander around and find things. She found empty rooms to use, office furniture, and organized a clothes closet.

Every month there was an "all community" meeting that was held at the dining hall on the first Wednesday night at seven o'clock. It was a celebration of student successes. Students would be recognized for sobriety goals, completing classes, getting a driver's license, finishing vocational training, or finding work, and the case managers would pass out certificates of recognition. They would play a game called Name that Tune, where the winner would get a twenty-dollar gift certificate. "It was a great atmosphere and a lot of fun, and it never felt like work at all." After a few years, Mariann would start the all-community meeting with music playing and a basket of candy. "If you dance with me, you can have some candy," she would proclaim as she danced around the room. How many of you can imagine putting yourself in this position? It was during this time that she introduced the Student of the Month award and abandoned the Name that Tune game because the same people were always winning. Student of the Month became an important staple in our program for both the students and the staff and usually included some lively debates among staff members.

It wasn't all fun and games at all of the meetings. Every other month the Community Action Committee (the CAC board) from the city of Rancho Cordova would attend a meeting at Mather for an update on the programs. They would ask for statistics on occupancy, jobs, and the status of our wait list, and they always wanted to hear about successful completions. On at least one occasion, staff had to justify to the CAC board a raise in rent to the students who were working. The students were up in arms over the increase, but with rising program costs at Mather, as presented by Mariann, the increase was approved. Students would often show up to the meetings and provide their input on important topics or areas of concern. Generally, there was a good working relationship with the CAC board, the students, and the staff at Mather. Members of the CAC board would often have information regarding city events that students and the children in the family programs could attend for recreation. Overall, the students and the staff worked together for the betterment of Mather Campus. This was an important lesson in community service for the students. The student who was the president of the Student Resident Council sat on the CAC board during his or her tenure. Often, being president of the Resident Council started out as a personality contest but ended up with the individual taking the responsibility seriously once they got involved.

Like all of us, Mariann recalls many people who came to Mather of whom her first reaction was "This one has very little chance to make it through." This included people with addictions who had spent several years living on the street and people who had spent significant time in jail or had endured other extremely difficult times in their life. But on most occasions, those people thrived at Mather, graduated, and are still doing amazingly overall. Mariann had four employees who were assigned to develop employment plans for the Mather students. They worked with the case managers and the job coach to assess the students, develop employment plans, and then track their progress with the student's case manager.

The service providers responsible for the students' case management and the staff of the Sacramento County DHA would meet every Monday, after our launch meeting, to discuss all matters of the students' progress. We would share the issues of concern, discuss options, and map out next steps. The goal was to keep all students on track to complete the program within the allotted time. On Thursdays, we would conduct a tour of potential new clients, where a group of approximately twelve clients would actually tour the campus and hear about the program elements. Mariann would always address the group early in the day and tell them, "This is an employment program. You're here to prepare for employment and get a job and move out." It was only after that statement she would go on to explain the services DHA supplied and answer questions about the program. DHA staff and the service provider's staff would conduct interviews in the afternoon, after the students had filled out applications and completed the campus tour. Interviews were done with teams of two to three staff members. We usually had six teams, and each team would complete two interviews on Thursday. After the interviews were completed and the potential clients had left, we would discuss each individual and as a group to determine whether or not to offer them a place in the program, subject to their background checks. Mariann was a vocal leader in all of these discussions.

DHA managed a Community Services Block Grant (CSBG) that was awarded to Mather. The funds were used to pay for vocational training, work tools, work clothes, and a program we called the Benchmark program. Students could earn money that was held until they graduated by completing certain milestones (benchmarks) in the program. There were three milestones, each worth $150, for a potential total of $450. Students were required to complete 192 hours of community service work. When they completed that work, they were awarded their first benchmark. Benchmarks were also awarded for completing vocational training and getting a job. Early in the program there was extra money in the CSBG that was used to fix the teeth of many of the students—teeth that had been lost or damaged from using methamphetamines. Students had to complete the program and leave without owing money to get their benchmark money.

Mariann actually started at Mather when DHA was the operating manager of the program. She was working for the campus director, and the work she did was not always in the framework that was represented in this profile. In 2009, the county chose to contract the overall management of Mather Campus and completed that through a public bid process that ended up being awarded to Volunteers of America (VOA). Having made that disclaimer, the process and the scope of work that was being done prior to change in management did not change significantly. After VOA assumed the operations management for the single site, Mariann moved over to the employment side and managed her team and their operation from the One-Stop job center located on campus. Overall, I had the pleasure of working with Mariann for 5 of the 11 years she worked at Mather.

Mariann seemed to know the name and the personal situation of every client on campus, month in and month out. This was no minor feat, with 183 singles on campus, and 10–12 leaving every month, replaced by new students. They all knew that she was one person who would help them with every ounce of energy she could muster if the need was real and they were working the program to the best of their ability. They also knew she was not a person who could be fooled with a sad story or an excuse. The Mather programming was being dismantled when Mariann left. She had put in her time with the county and now had grandchildren to spoil. I'm not sure she would have left if we had the public support to keep things together out there. She would tell you she was leaving anyway, but it wasn't fun for her anymore and that was a shame.

Meet Chris Mann (Staff)

I had intended to start these staff stories with Chris Mann for a couple of reasons. First, he has spent more time at Mather Community Campus as part of a service provider team than anyone. Second, he has worked in more positions hoping to improve the lives of homeless clients than anyone else there, and by default he has impacted the lives of more people than anyone I know. I can say that because Chris has dedicated his life to creating opportunities that very few others might see, let alone take on the challenge of implementing. And it was for a population with a lot of barriers in the way of their success.

Ultimately, Chris's story was inserted here because of the remarkable connection that he shared with the first two clients in the next chapter. Those clients, through bizarre circumstances, connected with each other and with Chris to participate in a fascinating adventure. It included three people who overcame addiction, two of whom were homeless and had spent time in jail. Truly random events led them to reach beyond anything that would be considered likely for people struggling to get through a local homeless reintegration program. I hope we capture a little of the "awe" in telling their stories and sharing this connection.

Chris Mann took his first job, with Volunteers of America, right out of high school in 1986, working with the children of inmates in prison. At that time, he was trying to work his way through his own alcohol and drug addiction, so he left the position and went back to college. It took him 9 years to get through college while fighting his addictions, and he finally got sober for good in 1995. He actually started working in social services again in 1994, helping juvenile sex offenders at a recovery home. He worked in the home and in the schools. He left that job and got sober with help from AA, where he learned and developed some incredible tools. He had a friend at AA who took him under her wing and told him, "We're going to go to meetings and conventions together, and you're going learn how to shake hands and kiss babies" (like he was running for president or something). Chris's main objective at the time was to avoid being alone. Through that process, even though he was very uneasy, he learned how to get comfortable with meeting new people and built some solid new habits. He had a sponsor who had him pick up cigarette butts and clean ashtrays at the meetings. He told his sponsor he didn't smoke, but his sponsor told him this is not about you, it is about doing whatever it takes to say sober. So, he did whatever his sponsor suggested. These interactions continued to strengthen his sobriety.

In 1997, Chris's mother mentioned that she had heard from a friend that VOA was hiring for a new program serving homeless people out at Mather Air Force Base. Chris applied for the job and was asked to come out for an interview. He managed to get hired and started on July 25, 1997. VOA had taken over a contract from another provider, who had literally left the site a few months earlier. There were forty-two single clients who had not had structured services for a few months and were unhappy with the situation. The program quickly grew to ninety clients. The clients were very apprehensive around the new guy. Chris chose to hang out at the dining hall and start out just by saying hello and introducing himself during the dining hours. It was his way of getting to know the students and to start building relationships. It was fairly volatile at that time on the campus, with some violence and drugs. The police were coming out on a regular basis, and a lot of people needed help.

Chris realized that the population was not very strong on social skills, so in addition to helping out with the classes, AA meetings, and running AA groups, Chris looked for a way to add more physical activities in the program. He had lost 50 pounds after he had gotten sober, with diet and sports exercise. He was looking for a way to add those principles into the programming along with the principles of recovery. Chris had become an avid soccer player. Soccer had kept him attached to the rest of the world during his addiction, and was a key activity for him in getting fit later. One day he was approached by the DHA director on campus, who asked him to take a ride with her. She started by saying they needed to find bicycles for the students, and then said, "What I really want is for you to develop a recreation program." With that encouragement, he started a tennis team and a golf team along with a leadership training program and a resident council that would have a voice in the operation of the programs at Mather. He later decided he wanted to start a volleyball program. Knowing that the county wouldn't approve it, he asked the landscape maintenance team to dig out an area he had marked up and to set two posts. This was done on a Thursday. On the following Saturday, he had some friends, with their truck, deliver sand. The following Monday, Mather had a volleyball court.

Chris had a client who we'll call Mike who had some criminal violence in his background. He would sit in Chris's office day after day. Chris finally asked him, "What do you want to do?"

Mike said, "I just don't want to put my hands on anyone."

Chris told him, "Well, you can't just sit here day after day."

"I'd really like to play softball," replied Mike.

With that motivation, Chris organized and created a softball team using old equipment the Air Force had left in storage at Mather. The City of Rancho Cordova even let the Mather team play in their adult league at no cost. They lost every game their first year. The team began to practice in their off season. By the end of the third year, they were not only winning games, but they had almost one hundred residents from the campus, singles and families with their children, out at the field rooting for their team. They were out there with pompoms and signs. There were fifteen men on that first softball team. Thirteen of those first fifteen players were a part of the first Mather graduating class. In the next few years, a recreation room was developed in the building that housed the old noncommissioned officer's club. Chris had gotten a donated pool/ping pong table and some used furniture for that space. The process of building a community with common goals, including social activities, was now well underway.

As an additional benefit to having a softball team, the Mather program was able to establish its presence in the community and develop relationships with local businesses. These were relationships that Chris was later able to leverage for additional support. Staff would do a clothing drive and these businesses began to donate a lot of really nice used clothing to the program's clothes closet. Chris talked about two businesses in particular, Sprint and Franklin Templeton, who had two thousand employees working in the area. He would go over with large laundry carts and they would fill them up with their donations. The students would later separate and hang the clothes in their clothes closet. Chris made another connection with an employee of Linens and Things, who ended up donating a bunch of goods with small imperfections from five different stores. Chris continued to collect all of these goods. Nothing got thrown out. He put it all in bins on the campus, and it eventually got to the students. Over a period of time the students ended up with carpeting and matching drapes, Nautica comforters, and other things they had never enjoyed before. These kinds of relationships with community partners would have a major impact on the programs at Mather over the years, including some incredibly generous ones. Some of them are recounted in the final chapter.

Chris got married in 2005 and decided he needed to leave VOA for a job with better pay to support his family. He ended up helping a friend build a direct mail business during that time and worked to complete his education in business matters. He came back to the agency in 2008, working with former foster youth. He did that for 18 months and then accepted the position of case manager back in the Mather singles program.

One evening in 2008, Chris was watching ESPN at home. On this particular show, there was an advertisement (one of only two times it was ever shown) about a homeless world street soccer tournament in South Africa. Chris became obsessed with getting Mather students the chance to participate in this tournament, and he posted signs to start a team. The one individual who he hoped would not sign up because he was just so angry, was of course the first person who signed up for the team. That was Jack. Remember Jack from the beginning of the book? Chris put together a team and managed to get seven players to compete. They would have to raise money and travel to Washington, DC, to compete in the national tournament. Certain players from the national tournament would be selected from around the country to represent the US in the homeless world street soccer tournament, which was to be held in Milan, Italy, the next year. Chris managed to raise the money, with the first check coming from Darrell Steinberg, who is now the mayor of Sacramento.

None of these street soccer players from Sacramento had ever been on a plane before, let alone competed in a national tournament. Several of them were on parole. They held a practice the day before the trip, and there was local news coverage to report on what was taking place and to meet the team. Chris knew if just one person could make the national team, they could come back to Sacramento and share their story. Well, they ended up going to DC, and one player was picked from the Mather team to go to Milan, Italy. That one player was Jack. When Jack came back from Milan, Chris picked him up at the airport. He told Chris, "I have to show you what I brought back." He opened up a big suitcase on the hood of Chris's car and it was filled with different items from around the world. He told Chris that he and the players had stayed in a large Red Cross tent. Jack had taken his best clothes to Milan from home. One of his neighbors, in the tent, was a goat farmer from Africa and he realized that if he gave that man his Nike shoes, he could feed his family for one week. He ended up giving everything he had to other players and bringing back stuff that had little monetary value but tremendous emotional value to him.

The following year, Jack became the coach. That same year, Chris recruited another player from Mather to participate, a woman whom you will meet in a few pages named Lisa. She had played soccer for Sacramento State University, but after years of struggling with life showed little interest in playing again. She ended up coming to a practice and got hooked. Chris and Lisa ended up going to the national tournament. Lisa was selected for the national women's team and Chris got selected to coach the men's team. They ended up going together that year to Rio de Janerio, Brazil, where Lisa would compete in the homeless world street soccer tournament. It is very difficult in a few paragraphs here to convey the magnitude of the events that unfolded as a result of one person's initiative. Chris began by trying to expand the vision and experience of a few homeless individuals. He introduced them to soccer just to get some exercise and pass the time that had previously been taken up with alcohol- and drug-related activity. These people not only represented their nation in international events, but as you will see, Jack and Lisa have moved on and continue to impact hundreds of disenfranchised people with their own passion to make a difference. Amazing things can happen when we add a little caring to another person's life. You never know what will be passed on into the future as a result of acts of kindness today. We just have to continue to create the environments where it can happen.

During Chris's tenure at Mather as a case manager and the recreation specialist, he had the opportunity to interact with local business at a few different levels. He had been accumulating charitable donations for clothing and housing supplies. He had interacted with other companies through the softball team during the league play. Plus, he had done fundraising for the development, outfitting, and travel of the world street soccer team from Sacramento. He was beginning to make the connection that there was much more value that could be realized from these and other business relationships for the employment opportunities of the Mather clients.

Over the next several years, Chris spent most of his time continuing to develop relationships with these businesses. He was able to develop a deeper understanding of their hiring processes, cultures, and requirements for new hires. Chris was able to work with a few of the larger and medium-size businesses in the area to understand their hire and pre-hire programs, and was able to successfully negotiate the rights to do the pre-employment screening for dozens of potential applicants who were Mather clients. After the prescreening was completed, they were ready to be interviewed by the personnel directors of these companies. On one occasion he organized a hiring event at Mather for a light manufacturing company that was looking to hire seasonal employees to assist in the startup of a new facility. There were thirty-nine candidates who had been prescreened; thirty-four of those candidates ended up getting hired. Overall, Chris helped more than one hundred Mather students get hired at that firm over an 18-month period.

This experience became a new launching pad for Chris and his vision to help all people reach new heights through employment. Chris has since worked in four different programs assisting those hoping to find employment; he was successful in all four. The secret has been in the development of his business relationships. That has included getting to know the individuals in each organization who do the hiring and getting an understanding of the hiring system that each of them use to staff their organizations. Additionally, he has researched and implemented excellent screening tools for understanding each person's interest and skill set. The benefit of that work was the confidence that the personnel directors and hiring managers had in him. They knew they were getting good candidates to interview. Development of professional business relationships is rare in the social service world, particularly when it is based on the ability to find good employees among formerly homeless people.

Chris is not surprised by his success or the success of his clients. He believes that all men and women have untapped potential, especially those who have been homeless or incarcerated or disenfranchised in other ways. When their potential is unlocked for possibly the first time and their value is recognized, also maybe for the first time, it is a powerful motivator and verifier of a person's true capacity. Chris continues to work with local business and disenfranchised populations, looking for the opportunity to change lives. He has many remarkable stories about people in our community who he has worked with who are not only paying taxes but are now positively impacting many others.

Summarizing the Impact of Mather Staff

These three staff stories only scratch the surface of the depth of dedicated, remarkable people who worked at Mather and through their efforts changed the course of well over four thousand lives. I would be remiss if I didn't include a special acknowledgment to the seventy dedicated VOA employees, the county of Sacramento, and the other social service providers who worked at Mather. For most of the final 15 years, especially prior to some dramatic changes discussed later, there was very little employee turnover. I believe that can be attributed to the joy of not only doing a job well but also being a part of the group that lifted human potential far beyond our expectations year after year. It elicited joy, and it was manifested in the annual graduations that were held every June from 1998 through 2019. These graduation events were regularly attended by county officials, Mather staff, the students' friends, and alumni. In many cases, members of the students' families who had been alienated from them for a long time would attend.

In 2015, the Mather employment program was scheduled for a Supplemental Nutrition Assistance Program (SNAP) audit regarding the use of their funds for employment-related activities. Both state and federal auditors came to the campus and spent 2 weeks with our program. They reviewed files, financial records, program details, and outcomes. They also met with our staff and attended student classes and employment-related meetings. They interviewed most of the Mather staff, along with dozens of students. At a "wrap up" meeting a few weeks later, the head state auditor began the meeting by making this statement: "We audit thirty-four employment programs throughout the state of California that are receiving funds from SNAPs; thirty-three of those programs are Mather 'wannabes.'"

CHAPTER 10

Mather Alumni

THERE ARE LITERALLY HUNDREDS OF AMAZING STORIES ABOUT people who showed up at Mather with a lot of baggage and very few useful tools in their toolkits, and who left with a chance at a new life. I will highlight just a few here.

Jack: The Rest of the Story

We left Jack's story when he was leaving Folsom Prison, after being accepted in a residential alcohol and drug recovery program. He was there for only 12 days, and after beating up a resident over a dispute, he ran away again. He ended up going to the county alcohol and drug office and was able to secure a bed at VOA's Bannon Street Shelter. He didn't really understand recovery at this point, but he knew he couldn't go back to Folsom Prison. At this point, he was just starting recovery through AA's twelve-step program and taking anger management classes. While at Bannon Street, he had gotten on the wait list to come to Mather. In August of 2007, he got his interview there and was accepted into the program. He was working and agreed to quit his job to participate in the program requirements. Jack had a reputation that came with him to Mather. The support staff supervisor, during the first few days Jack was at Mather, approached him and said, "I have one big request of you at your time at Mather: Promise me you won't lay hands on any other students or staff." He agreed. That first summer at Mather was eventful. Jack's initial reaction was to complain that there were too many classes that he had to attend and too many meetings.

There were several life-changing events that took place in that summer of 2007. Jack now had a sponsor at AA. He was about to move to the third step that requires the participant to submit to a higher power. Jack was about to choose God. His sponsor had asked him to meet in McKinley Park. Part of the process of submitting to a higher power is to pray the prayer of acknowledgment. When he met up with his sponsor in the park, his sponsor said to him: "OK, let's get down on our knees and pray the prayer." Jack looked around and said, "Right here in the middle of the park?" "Yes" was the response. This became a defining moment for Jack. Surrendering to a higher power opened up an avenue to let other influences go to work in him. Back at Mather, he attended classes with a new outlook and began to acquire a new set of skills he had never had. He made himself vulnerable to the whole community and the program.

At his AA meetings, he had begun the process of rethinking past prejudices that had been honed in prison. His twelve-step support group was mostly African Americans. He attended all of his meetings with the staff counselors and began to realize that the entire staff was there to help him through the program. He was now a part of a community and had a network of support for the first time in his life. Jack immersed himself in his new environment. While he was settling in at Mather, his father was dying of liver failure. He had moved to Idaho and there was not much communication. Jack was on parole at the time and put in a request to go see his father; but as a level-4 parolee, he was denied. His dad died in February 2008, and Jack told his parole officer he was going to the funeral regardless of the consequences. His dad died on the 1-year anniversary of Jack's sobriety. Jack told me the family gathered at a bar after the funeral. He went with them and remained sober.

After a few months back at Mather, Jack received a certificate of recognition for keeping his room clean. I heard him speak at a Mather alumni meeting years later and he talked about how important it was to receive that first certificate. It was the first time anyone had outwardly recognized him for good work. He had never gotten any recognition at home. He still has that certificate, along with several others he received during his stay at Mather. He took a CPS-approved parenting class that became a ticket for him to start supervised visits with his children. He spent time with the employment services team and learned how to put together a resume, how to interview, and how to dress to seek employment. He started wearing a dress shirt and tie to the dining hall and his classes.

Jack had also immersed himself in the sports and recreation programs at Mather and was the first person to sign up for Chris Mann's homeless street soccer team. This is where he got his first exposure to the importance of and the opportunities that come through team dynamics. When Jack returned from Milan with a suitcase full of stuff that had little monetary value, he didn't realize the symbolism of the exchange he had made with the other players. That "stuff" would end up being a testimonial to the changes happening in his life.

The following year, Jack became the coach of the local street soccer team that Chris had started. He continued to facilitate practices and took a team back to Washington, DC, twice and to New York once for the national tournament.

During his time at Mather, Jack started attending college. He was able to secure an interview with a parole agent for a position with AmeriCorps. Since he did not have a resume with work history, he took the certificates he had accumulated at Mather with him. He was offered a position with AmeriCorps and started working with youth on parole who were trying to turn their lives around. Jack eventually met a girl he trusted, and with his new job, he moved out of Mather in 2009. He spent 5 years facilitating groups at juvenile hall and talked about how the experience of walking through the yard as an instructor instead of a felon was surreal.

Jack is married now and continues to work in social services helping others restore their lives. He is still involved in supporting the homeless street soccer program. He has gone from a convict to a facilitator to a parent. He has a solid relationship with both of his children, who are now a part of his everyday life. His daughter is now 20 years old and his son is 18. His relationship with God has continued to grow and is now a foundation stone in his life. He will tell you that being sober is not a goal; it is also a foundation stone to everything else in his life. Chris Mann and Jack remain good friends. They go out to the river on weekends during the winter and distribute socks to the homeless. We cannot reveal Jack's current employer, but he continues to serve the homeless, helping them locate services, housing options, and work. He has been active and impactful in this work for the last 5-plus years. Jack will tell you that Mather and God saved his life.

A final note on Jack: We need to remember that at 13 years old Jack was homeless, committing crimes, using drugs, and not attending school. No one bothered to look for him or to try and figure out what he was doing. The idea that there is no one in the world who cares for you is an isolating, cold revelation that has major underlying impacts on a developing young man and his image of the world. Without help that involves kindness and caring from others, that journey of moving away from a life of crime is very difficult and may be impossible.

Meet Lisa Wrightsman (Student)

More times than I can remember, someone would show up who was homeless at the time, who just seemed out of place waiting to be interviewed in the Mather conference room. I do have to admit, I was not at Mather when Lisa Wrightsman showed up to apply, but having met her and having personally witnessed her speaking to a future graduating class, I recognized this was another person who, had I known about her life growing up, I would never have guessed would end up in a homeless transitional housing program. But that does prove a point. Life can deal out harsh realities to anyone when you least expect it. We have a saying in our organization in regard to this reality: "There but for the grace of God go I." I have been studying human behavior and development in relation to trauma for several years. I have learned that as humans, we have a very difficult time feeling safe and secure if we allow ourselves to truly believe that the world can be random when it comes to tragedy. If we are smart and if we are good people and have some level of street smarts, we can protect ourselves from those devastating issues that impact our careless counterparts. If we did not feel this way, we would have a hard time going out and climbing our mountains every day. But tell that to earthquakes, floods, random acts of violence, nightclub shootings, or prescription drugs that turn to addictions. There are hundreds of people every year who find themselves in desperate situations, trying to figure out what happened to them along the way. Lisa was one of them.

Lisa is a remarkable person. She is a leader in our community and does terrific work with underprivileged women in the community. Lisa told me she grew up middle class, but after a pause, she said it felt more like lower class. Her parents divorced and she ended up seeing her father only on weekends. He remarried but struggled with depression and other mental health-related issues. Her mother worked, so Lisa spent a lot of time with babysitters and did not have much after-school discipline. Lisa was always gifted athletically, and sports became her everyday relief. "Sports made me feel safe, included, and normal." But, at 12 years old she was diagnosed with cancer. She had to endure 4 months of aggressive chemo treatments and separation from her sports. During this treatment period, she felt emotionally isolated from her peers. She also had her first experience with opioids and morphine.

When the treatment was completed and she was declared free from cancer, it brought extreme relief. She felt her prayers had been answered by God and therefore she felt more personally responsible. She also felt invincible and ready to go. The experience with cancer gave Lisa a new perspective on life, one that was somewhat isolating and made reintegration into her teens a little difficult. Soccer became a big piece of her life during this time. When she was fifteen, she had her first alcoholic drink. In her words, this became the new answer to everything. She felt more connected and at ease, and this continued every week through high school. Her soccer led to a scholarship at Sacramento State University. Lisa made the decision to curb her drinking and focus on the soccer, and this allowed her to get through college. She did manage to get her bachelor's degree at Sacramento State, being a good athlete had protected her. She had been preparing to play women's professional soccer and was on the radar of the local franchise. She felt she was being groomed to play professional soccer. Unfortunately, shortly after she completed college, the women's professional soccer league folded and killed her dream.

After college, and without the goal of professional soccer available, she was ill-prepared to continue to be self-disciplined with substance abuse. She started drinking more, taking pain pills, and smoking marijuana. In 2005 Lisa got her first DUI. She swore she would never drink and drive again. Nine months later she got another DUI. She entered into the conversation on alcoholism, but she personally did not think her problems were about the power of alcohol. She found herself in 2008 trying to find work without a driver's license. She managed to stop drinking but ended up getting hooked on painkillers. "After all, you can't smell painkillers on someone's breath." It was costing her $200 per week to keep herself supplied. In 2009, Lisa tried methadone as way to get off the opioids. The withdrawals were very bad and she couldn't function. She then started using meth for the first time and she liked it ... a lot.

After the professional soccer dream had been lost, Lisa worked as a personal trainer and played semi-professional soccer, hoping to go professional. Her last professional tryout was in 2008. Trying to figure out what to do after soccer, she started using meth heavily. She eventually lost her job, and the economy in general was in the tank. There was no structure in Lisa's life and she began to entertain conspiracy theories, never thinking that meth was the real problem. She was in and out of jail six or seven times; sometimes for driving without a license, sometimes for a DUI, a failure to appear in court, or a payment missed. In any event, it was getting difficult to keep track.

The last time she was arrested, she was on her way to pay off a drug dealer. She had planned on not using that day but ended up buying more anyway. In a very bizarre set of circumstances, the police showed up and arrested her for robbery (mistaken identity), possession of drugs, and an outstanding bench warrant. Lisa says she actually felt a sense of relief. Reality had set in that she actually no longer knew how to function normally. Her mother refused to bail her out this time. Her mother did agree a little later to help her get into an alcohol and drug rehabilitation facility. She went and had her first adult experience with sobriety. She says this was a very significant event, as it was her first time meeting people who understood how she felt. It gave her new hope to find someone who "finally understood." Lisa was learning how to communicate and how to hear other people's stories. She loved the experience of sharing, while learning how hard it was for women to open up. She loved going to AA meetings, and while in rehab, she was placed on the waiting list to come to Mather Campus. Shortly after her interview at Mather, she got the call that she had been accepted and would be moving into the facility in 1 week. "It felt like the opportunity of a lifetime."

Lisa moved in, got her own apartment with her own bathroom, and felt safe. That first night she wandered out on campus and got asked to play in a pickup volleyball game. That experience made her feel welcome and gave her a couple of new friends to eat meals with. She told her case manager, Chris Mann, that this was the first real chance in her life to rediscover herself. While Lisa was at Mather, she finished her DUI classes, got her license back, and was able to improve her credit and learn how to financially manage a household. She maintained her sobriety and worked to pay off her student loans. With Chris's help, she got a job at Asher College in Sacramento. Chris asked Lisa if she might be interested in participating in street soccer. She said her first reaction was no, but when she went out to the grounds during a practice session and started kicking a soccer ball around with fellow students (who were way below her skill level), she just fell in love with the experience.

The remaining parts of this story are almost too good to be true. Lisa ended up playing street soccer here in Sacramento while at Mather and made her way to a national tournament in Washington, DC. This opened her eyes more fully to what she could do with her life. It made the whole idea of sobriety much more exciting: "If this is what sobriety is all about, then I am all in." Being able to rebuild broken lives without embarrassment and seeing the success of other addicts was extremely motivating. In Washington, DC, she was recognized for her soccer talent and her character and got an invitation to play in the homeless world street soccer tournament in Brazil.

Upon her return to Sacramento, Lisa resumed her full-time employment at Asher College, where she worked for 5 years. At Mather, she had completed the "Ready to Rent" program, improved her credit report, and she had sobriety and the motivation to stay sober in hand. With these assets and the benchmark money she had earned at Mather, she was able to move into her own apartment. She began working on the development of a women's street soccer program with a question at the back of her mind: "How do I make this a full-time job?" Lisa realized that soccer could provide motivation to many women who got involved and were living on the streets. It motivated the women (and their children) to stay sober. Women bringing children to the soccer program actually improved the program. Lisa worked from 2010 through 2018, making Women's Street Soccer her full-time job. In 2016, she received support from the Sacramento County Board of Supervisors and partnered with the City of Sacramento. She was also doing grassroots fundraising for Women's Street Soccer. Eventually, she would get a financial commitment from UC Davis for support and raise additional money through grants. She has since hired additional full-time help from people who were street soccer mothers/players in her program and has gone on to become a national and international spokesperson for this growing social service program.

Lisa still talks about the fundamental skills she learned at Mather Community Campus that have continued to benefit her, in addition to the barriers she overcame at Mather that she revealed in this story:

- The importance of sobriety;

- Time management;

- Community support;

- The development of a personal skill set.

As she puts it, Lisa "came back to God" in the second step of her AA program. She is getting married in the near future and continues to bless our homeless population and our community. Lisa overcame some very difficult circumstances and now continues to help change the landscape of the lives of many women. Who knows the impact those women will have on other people needing help in the future? The whole process of people "paying back" their community and their fellow citizens is one of the most important untold stories in the life of people who manage to exit homelessness. It is another huge benefit that is at risk, in the new paradigm of homeless services, going forward.

Meet Nicki (Student)

Nicki was a single mom living on the streets with her two children, both under 10 years old. She was living in a car and moving from driveway to driveway, addicted to drugs, with no plan or picture for her future or the future of her children. It did not take long for her to lose her children. She was in and out of jail and medical facilities, without a permanent place to live. She had been relying on the welfare money she received for her children and herself and food stamps to get by for years. When she lost her children, the welfare money dwindled and so did a part of Nicki. She managed to get into a substance abuse recovery program and after 3 months was referred to Mather Community Campus.

The last time we spoke to Nicki, she was finishing her 13th year as a program manager for a major social service provider in our community. She remains clean and sober. She had earned her bachelor's degree and was, in 2019, working on a master's degree in social services. She got her children back while she was at Mather. Now she is a tax-paying, hardworking, necessary citizen giving back to her community and changing the lives of hundreds, if not thousands, of disenfranchised people. This is one of hundreds of stories that came out of Mather Campus.

Meet Mike (Student)

Mike is a middle-aged African American male. He was homeless from 1997 to 2004. He lost his job before becoming homeless, mostly due to his struggle with alcohol and drugs. He couched surfed, lived on the street, and collected unemployment until it ran out. He then collected general assistance, got on food stamps, and used the system for as long as he could. Finally, when he needed more money, he became a shoplifter, committing crimes to support his addiction. After a number of relapses, he reached out for help and was able to get to Mather in 2004.

He tells us he found support, structure, continuity, and community through the Mather program. He learned how to contribute to a community and use the support to abate his addiction. He also learned how to get ready to go back to work. He was able to get a job in 2005 while at Mather, and he is still working for the same company. He became a homeowner in 2009 and still stays in contact with fellow Mather alumni today. He is grateful for his second chance and acknowledges that many people never get that in life. For 15 years, he has paid income taxes and sales taxes in his community; and he has paid real estate taxes for over 10 years. More importantly, today he feels like he is a solid citizen contributing in his community.

There are hundreds of Mather stories like Mike's. These are people who continue to change the landscape of our entire community in Northern California.

Meet Sam Frank (student and staff member)

Sam is big man. He reaches about 6'5" and weighs close to three hundred pounds. He is in his late forties as I write this. He has been employed by VOA since 2012 as both a driver and a member of the support staff team. Sam is married (common law) to his wife Tina and they own a home in Rancho Cordova. They have one child, a 6-year-old boy named Daniel, who is the center of their universe. Daniel's first 6 years have been anything but ordinary. Diagnosed with a rare and aggressive disease that looked at one point like it might cost him his eyesight, Daniel has endured numerous tests and surgeries, some of which were experimental in nature. There were times when it looked as if Sam might have snapped from the stress and worry of those surgeries and their uncertain outcomes. But Sam and Tina made sure Daniel got the best medical care available, working with a world-class team at Stanford University Medical Center. Today Daniel is doing just fine, thank you. When you read the rest of Sam's story, you will see that everything beyond being above ground is remarkable, let alone being a trusted employee, homeowner, husband, and father.

Sam grew up in Sacramento County, spending his adolescent years with his maternal mother and father. Both parents were alcoholics, and eventually their marriage ended in divorce. Sam's dad remarried and Sam's new stepmother moved in. Between his dad's first marriage and his second marriage, Sam was the youngest of fifteen children: seven from his maternal mother and eight from his stepmother. From the time his stepmother moved in, she was physically abusive with Sam, beating him regularly and often severely. He actually didn't fully understand how abnormal this was until he had his own son. Somewhere in his teenage years, he became significantly bigger than his stepmom and the beatings stopped. When he was 11, one of his older stepbrothers introduced him to speed, and it wasn't long until he was hooked. He started recreational drinking after that, and at age 15 a friend introduced him to meth to help with a hangover. He became addicted and continued to use meth for the next 15 years. During that time, he bounced back and forth between his mom and dad. His mom continued her drinking and his stepmother remained cruel. During his sophomore year in high school, Sam took a severe fall and broke his right leg in nine places. He ended up not finishing high school. He left home and stayed at his sister's home for a while. Sam got his first job washing dishes at McClellan Air Force Base when he was 17.

He later took a job at a toy store at Arden Mall and moved into his own apartment. He switched jobs at the mall and ended up selling jewelry for few years. He was pretty good at that job and made enough money to keep his apartment and party heavily during this period. He left that job and started cleaning pools on his own. A few years rolled by, and Sam met his first wife at the age of 26. They got married and she moved into his apartment. They later moved together into a duplex in South Sacramento and Sam took a job at a hardware store. She was working two jobs at that time, while Sam's continued use of drugs and alcohol finally resulted in his becoming unemployed. Sam was arrested for the first time—a DUI charge. He continued to party while she worked. Eventually, she tired of that arrangement and left Sam. He was 28 years old and unemployed. He was eventually evicted from his residence because he couldn't pay the rent. He would find himself living on the street for the next 8 months.

Sam had a cousin who invited him to come to Oklahoma to stay with him for a time. He accepted the offer and soon got a job working in another hardware store. While he was there, he was able to stop using meth, but he was smoking marijuana and drinking. He was soon arrested for the second time on a possession charge. After a few years there, Sam's mother contacted him; his grandmother had passed away and she wanted him to come live with her. His mother had been living with his grandmother in Salt Lake City. Sam went there to live with her and soon got a job working at a gas station. They stayed there for 2 years, where Sam continued to smoke pot and drink. When Sam was 30, he and his mother moved back to Sacramento. She had stopped drinking, but Sam was still partying all the time. After some time, he moved back in with his dad and stepmother. One of Sam's older brothers influenced him to start using meth again, and from that point on, his life spiraled out of control. It was 2002, and Sam would spend the next 6 years addicted to meth and homeless.

Homeless people can end up being nomadic, and that was the case for Sam. He lived for over 6 months in a cemetery, climbing over the wall where the earth-moving equipment was kept each night and sleeping in, on, or underneath the equipment. He told me it was a good place to be homeless. There were not any people at night and it was quiet and relatively safe. He lived in a field behind the army depot for 3 years, scraping up tarps and old tents for cover. For a period of time, he was able to sleep on one of his cousin's couches. He met his current wife while he and his cousin were at a drug house doing a drug deal. They got together, and Sam and Tina found their next temporary home at a youth detention facility that had closed. Sam admits to deconstructing a large part of the interior of that building to get the copper out of the walls and other materials they could sell to survive.

They eventually had to move out of the detention facility, and they next took up residence in a Tough Shed sales display behind a Home Depot store. It was 2 months before they were discovered and had to leave. At that point, Tina called her brother for help, and he was able to get her a county-funded bed at a residential alcohol and drug treatment facility. Sam stayed out on his own for 3 more months, but his loneliness and his extremely high tolerance to drugs forced him to seek help. With some help from Tina and her brother, he was able to get a bed at the Bannon Street Shelter, which was run by VOA. He told me that on his way to the shelter, he had a pocket full of drugs and a drug pipe. He hid them in the dirt behind a bush. His plan was to check in, get his bed, and come back and retrieve his drugs.

He did check in and get his bed. But on his way back to retrieve his drugs, he experienced an ominous feeling that something had to change and change quickly. When he got back to the place where he had hidden his drugs, they were gone. Sam took that as sign from above that he had to give up the meth for good or there would be no future. Sam met his first true mentor at Bannon Street. She was the assistant director and helped Sam get his new start. He was required to attend recovery meetings for 90 days in a row in order to stay.

During Sam's first month at Bannon Street, Tina had been referred to Mather Campus by her service provider and had begun the program. Sam completed his required recovery meetings. When he had completed those 90 days, he was put on the wait list to get into Mather. After 6 months at Bannon Street, Sam got an interview and the call that he had been accepted into the Mather program. Sam told me he cried like a baby when he got that call. He cried because he knew it was the only real chance he had to start a new life. He will tell you that the first 4 to 6 months at Mather were very busy and challenging. He finished his required 6 weeks of classes, 160 hours of community service, and recovery meetings, and took advantage of the other services that were available. He took the "Ready-to-Rent" classes and met with the credit specialist who "performed miracles," as he put it. He had no idea what kind of training or work he might do, but with help from his case manager and the employment services team, he was able to get into a Class A driver's license training program. He showed up at Mather not having a driver's license and left with a Class A license and a job driving commercial trucks for food delivery. Sam and his wife left Mather together after he had finished 18 months in the program.

Sam's new job was just a few miles from Mather, so Sam would stop in regularly to visit staff. Two years after he had left, there was a position for a driver/support staff person that opened at Mather. Greg Williams encouraged Sam to apply, and he became a VOA employee at Mather in 2012. He still works for one of the agency's family programs that is operating at Mather. We shared Sam's current personal life status at the beginning of this profile to show just how far he has come in his life. To many of us, he is a Mather miracle. What we didn't share is the heartache that he now has over the dismantling of the employment programs at Mather. The last thing he said to me at our interview was, "To me, Mather was and always will be sacred ground."

Meet Jenna Winn (Student and Staff Member)

The last question that I asked Jenna at the end of our 2-hour interview was: "Why did you apply to come work at Mather Campus?" She told me that she loved Mather Campus and what it had meant to her life. She said that until she got to Mather, she had no idea that she could build the life she is currently enjoying. There had been nothing, prior to entering the program, that made her believe she could have a family, a home, and a job that was free from violence, drugs and alcohol, and the fear that is constantly attached to living on the streets and committing crimes. "I owe Mather my life," she said. I have heard this several times before, and it is expressed in a few of the stories shared here. Let that sink in for a moment. It is the most basic motivation I have for getting this work published. Because there is nothing in our community today that comes close to what Mather did—equipped people with the tools to make a life they never dreamed of before this program. And there have been a few thousand people who got that chance at Mather and capitalized on it.

But let's take a look at what Jenna's life was prior to coming to Mather and thank her for the courage and honesty to share her story. Jenna's early childhood was spent with her mother and stepfather. Both parents were drug addicts and her stepfather was physically abusive with her mother. By the time Jenna was 8 years old, she was stealing money to feed herself. When her stepfather found out, he threatened to shoot her with his shotgun. That was enough for her to leave the household. She bounced around for a couple of years, living with her older sister for a while, her older brother for a while, her godmother, and her aunt. At the age of 11, Jenna was raped by her aunt's husband. He visited her room more than once, and she kept a journal of the experiences. It was soon after this experience that she started using methamphetamines. At school, during a sex education class, she shared these experiences with her teachers, who wasted little time in contacting the authorities. Although her aunt's husband vehemently denied any involvement, he ended up going to prison and Jenna ended up in foster care. She was returned to her parents when she was 13 years old.

After returning to her parents, she started hanging out with kids who were older than she. Through those new relationships, she started selling meth. Her stepfather continued to be abusive with her mother, and her relationship with him became very confrontational. After a few years, she would have her first experience with being incarcerated. She was arrested for check fraud and sent to juvenile hall. Not too long after she was released, at age 17, she moved to Michigan. By the time she was 18, she was back in California. She soon got arrested for second-degree burglary and an outstanding warrant and was sent to the Sacramento County jail. Upon her release in 2004, she hooked up with a gang and started stealing cars and selling meth. She was arrested again and charged with forty-seven counts of grand theft auto (GTA). She was convicted on one of the charges and spent 90 days in the county jail again in 2005. After she was released, she was arrested again for GTA and spent 6 months in the county jail. In 2006, she was convicted a third time for GTA in Sacramento County, along with a conviction in Placer County for second-degree burglary.

By this time, her stepfather had passed away. Jenna was diagnosed with a mental health condition and started taking Wellbutrin. Eventually, she was arrested for evasion of parole, and as a three-time felon, she was sentenced to spend 2 years in the state penitentiary. An additional 8 months was added for the Placer County burglary charge. She was discharged in 2008 under Senate Bill 1453 with a requirement to attend residential substance abuse treatment for 6 months. While in treatment, she met several people who told her she should apply for the transitional housing program at Mather. Not knowing a thing about the program, she ignored the recommendations.

When Jenna left the residential treatment facility after 6 months, she was truly homeless as an adult for the first time. She spent much of the following year sleeping in stolen cars and not knowing where she was going to sleep next. She was getting high, and after spending a winter night in a stolen car, without any warm clothes, she decided she needed to go back to prison. She got arrested for another stolen car and was back in prison in 2010. She was released in 2011 and ended up back in the same residential treatment center. This time, Jenna took the advice of her peers and counselors and got her name on the wait list for Mather Campus. She was number 394 on their list. As an addict in recovery, with a substantial criminal record and no work history, Jenna was not a marketable commodity in the community. Her prospects looked very dim for escaping the only life she had really known, which was dominated by drugs and crime.

She got into Mather in 2012. Jenna will tell you it was an amazing experience from the first day. It was the first time that she had ever had her own apartment. It was the first time she was a part of a community of her peers who were also working on improving their lives. She immersed herself in the program and took all the classes, met with the credit specialist, and worked on cleaning up her criminal record. She was hired in the campus intern training program for building maintenance. For the first time in a very long time, she felt safe and knew that there were people who cared about her. She completed the program (which allowed a stay of up to 2 years at the time), got a job, and moved out in 13 months.

Jenna worked as a telemarketer through 2014 ("I was really good at it"). She then took an advertising position in her brother's plumbing company. She got pregnant during this time and took a maternity leave. She came back to visit the staff at Mather, and someone suggested she apply for a support staff position with VOA on campus. She did and worked at the campus until the singles program was closed in December 2019. She is still employed with VOA as a case manager in a different program. She has been helping others recast their vision and achieve things they once thought were impossible. Jenna is now married and raising two daughters, who are at the center of her new life. Jenna has been mourning the closure of the Mather transitional housing program. It gave her the life she never could have envisioned.

CHAPTER 11

The End of a Promising Era for the Homeless

YOU SHOULD HAVE A REASONABLY COMPLETE PICTURE OF the options for managing the homeless service issues that most communities have been working with over the past decade. I intended to show an effective option that was here locally and working through 2014 in the form of transitional housing. What followed was the push to Housing First, which started in earnest in our community in 2015. I have discussed what those programs offered as well as provided insight into some of the housing, sans service solutions, that is being discussed for the future. There has been more than one 10-year plan to end homelessness initiated in this community and others; but as reported, the "published" population of homeless continues to grow each year. The numbers we see are based on the point-in-time count that is done each year, which excludes several categories of homeless or imminently homeless people. This means that the actual numbers are much higher than those being reported.

It should also be noted that the pending impacts from the recent COVID-19 pandemic are going to further inflate the numbers soon. Unemployment has increased, especially among small business, and eventually the unemployment benefits will run out. Many of the small businesses forced to close will not be able to fully recover. Those problems will be compounded by what is happening, out of the spotlight, with landlords and mortgage companies that have been mandated to keep restrictions on evictions and foreclosures at this time. When these government restrictions on evictions end, more people will be forced to the street. With more people becoming homeless and fewer services available, there is little opportunity to move a significant part of this population to self-sufficiency.

This is the result of closing programs that offered the services needed to accomplish this goal (vocational training, employment, credit repair, substance abuse recovery, and barrier reduction). The Mather experiences of the last 20 years suggest that well over 50% of the homeless population could reach self-sufficiency in 2 years with the right programs. Instead, the services needed to make this happen have slowly been reduced or eliminated or are no longer considered relevant. In this chapter, we will highlight the things that caused the slow, deliberate, and thorough dismantling of a program that accomplished those goals for over 20 years prior to being closed.

Financial Review

There is probably more financial detail presented below than will be of interest to the average reader. It is being presented in detail to show, in this case, how a very successful and publicly popular homeless program was slowly taken apart. It was fueled by the removal of financial support over an extended period of time, for a variety of reasons. What is unclear is whether or not this financial obsolescence was planned for an extended period of time or it became a convenient option somewhere along the line. If you choose to read through it, you will get a detailed look at how the public funding of social programs works and, in the case of Mather, how the slow demise of a successful program happens outside of the public eye.

The following financial review is specific to historical events that took place in Northern California. I believe they are representative of the issues that have been highlighted in this book, specific to federal government control of local funding for homeless services. The example being presented here began with the federal policy changes for funding homeless services and shows the trickle-down impact that occurred locally, over a decade, from those policy changes. What we are left with reflects a troubling outlook for the homeless going forward. The actual figures presented here are from the internal budgets of Volunteers of America for Mather Campus. This information was shared on numerous occasions with county officials, and all of the financial records supporting county contracts were subject to numerous audits from the county auditors.

Budget

At one point, the annual budget for Mather Campus grew to $10 million. Clients could stay for up to 2 years at that time. The budget included all of the services and critical personnel that were listed in chapter 7, including the recreation programs. There were a number of service providers working together on-site. In addition to the county DHA One-Stop, VOA was managing the single site, Next Move was managing the family site, and Pride Industries (and later Crossroads) was the contractor for finding employment opportunities. My first year was 2014, and the funding budget for Mather had been reduced to a little over $6 million. Subsequent reductions in funding forced some changes to the management structure over time and eventually to the structure of the program. In 2014, we consolidated some of the programming and eliminated certain program elements to reduce the maximum stay from 2 years to 1 year. This effectively cut the cost, per student, by 30%.

HUD Funding and Reductions

In 2015, the HUD funding that supported the families at Mather was suspended, and was to be reallocated to other rapid rehousing programs in the community. VOA made an attempt to fill the financial hole with other family programs at Mather. It turned out that the new family program was difficult to assimilate there, and the funding fell $500,000 short of what had been in place. At that time, the total funding for the singles program was $4,191,450. There would be more funding reductions that crippled the program over the next 5 years. Table 2 tracks the financial reduction made from the federal, state, or county government contracts. They, in turn, caused service cuts to the program and a scramble to find alternative financing. The revenue cuts would continue with reductions to student fees that were explained away as more policy changes. Listed below are the actual annual reductions that were made year after year to the singles program. The years represented are the county fiscal year, which starts on July 1 of each year and ends on June 30. The first year shown below is 2014, which actually started on July 1, 2013. The number of single students being served stayed at 180 until December 2018, when the total was reduced to 140 to make room for 40 homeless veterans.

Table 2. Mather Campus annual funding and cost reductions.

Funding Year	Students Served	Funding Total ($)	Net Change ($)	Funding Per Student ($)	Cost Per Student ($)
2014	120	4,191,457		34,928	35,000
2015	180	4,009,495	−181,962	22,275	26,000
2016	180	3,993,030	−16,465	22,184	26,000
2017	180	3,810,961	−182,069	21,172	25,000
2018**	180	2,413,408	−1,397,283	13,407	20,000*
Subtotal			−1,777,779		
2019	180	2,169,164	−244,244	15,494	18,000
2020	140	1,443,094	−726,070	10,307	15,000
Grand total			−2,748,093		

*The "cost per student" was reduced through reductions in staff beginning in 2018.

**The final year the Mather Singles program received HUD funding.

Note. The "funding per student" calculation for 2014 is based on an average of 120 students, as this was the final year, Mather still had some students enrolled in a 2-year program. The calculations for 2015 through 2018 are based on serving 180 single students, and the calculations beginning 2019 (which started in July of 2019) are based on 140. Even though there were a total of 180 apartments for singles, in the years 2012–2019 we typically served closer to 200 because the average stay was a little less than 10 months. The number of students that was used for budgeting purposes was 180. The HUD funds for Mather Singles were $2,534,000 annually. After 2017–2018, the final year the program received HUD funding, the county passed a special funding measure to replace part of that loss with $1 million of county general funds. If you find this financial model difficult to follow, just focus on the difference between the funding received per student each year and the cost per student to run the program. The cost per student calculation is based on the simple calculation of actual dollars spent divided by the number served. There was substantial additional support that was generated through in-kind donations of goods and services through businesses and individuals that is not reflected in the financial analysis. All of that support left as the program was closing.

The cost per student to run the program in 2014 was approximately $35,000 per year. As shown in Table 2, the revenue coming in was very close to the cost to run the program. In 2014,

Mather was being transitioned from a 2-year program to a 1-year program. By 2015, the cost per student had been reduced to approximately $26,000 per year. Some of the gap between revenues and cost was absorbed by the in-kind donations of goods and services. There was also an additional grant in place that paid for vocational training. At the peak of the use of those grant funds, Mather benefited by around $400,000 per year or $2,222 per student. The balance of the annual deficits was made up through private fund raising or direct subsidy payments from VOA. From 2014 through 2017, the funding deficits fluctuated from $300,000 to $600,000 each year.

Funding Deficit and Emergency Funding Plan

In 2009, there had been a serious concern that Mather Campus would have a funding deficit that could not be filled and might be forced to close. There was a public hearing to discuss the closing of the campus. A very large contingent of the Mather students attended the public hearing to protest the action. They would ultimately help influence the final decision to keep the program open. An emergency-funding plan was put into place in 2010 that all invested parties (the county and the service providers) agreed to and that would sustain the project for several years. However, most of the additional revenue sources included in that plan were removed over the next few years after a review was completed by state auditors. The result was major losses of funding to the program. Eventually (2018), there was a legal demand from the county (originated at the state level) for VOA to reimburse a large sum of revenue that had been used for operations in prior years, revenue that had been approved as part of their emergency-funding plan.

By the end of 2019, the plans to offer the services needed to run an employment center and housing at Mather was a financial impossibility. *When VOA informed the county that due to the new funding limits, they could not meet the contract requirements, the county informed VOA they would cancel the contract effective December 2019 (halfway into the 2020 contract) and would rebid the program with new operating guidelines.* This was done through the RFP process (a public request for proposal). Except for negligible administrative adjustments, in the 10 or 11 years that VOA had managed the employment program at Mather, there had been no revenue increase in any of the contract amounts for inflation or cost of living increases. VOA was given the message during this time that there was nothing extra in the county general fund available to extend the program.

Request for Proposal Process

The first new RFP for services was put out for bid in October of 2019. It was a 6-month contract proposal to serve 140 clients. The dollar amount was $772,000. There were three providers who showed up for the bidders' conference (a requirement to bid the RFP). There were no guidelines for client services in the RFP other than the requirement to house the clients and provide three hot meals per day. Not a single service provider put in a bid for that contract at that amount. The county then put out an amended RFP with an increase in the contract amount to $1.5 million for 6 months.

When VOA did their analysis, this dollar amount still didn't cover the costs for 140 clients, and the lack of programming requirements provided very little opportunity for positive outcomes. Only one provider bid on the new RFP; it was later revealed that the bid from that provider only included serving 80 clients (one residential building out of the two that housed the singles). That agency was awarded the contract with the understanding that the county would take financial responsibility for case managing the remaining 60 clients. When the dust settled, in retrospect, this process converted one of the most successful homeless services programs (as measured by the number of people who were exiting homelessness) into a 140-bed shelter, with virtually no services. There is nothing in the history of the county RFP process, that I am aware of, where a bidder has been allowed to reduce the number of clients and client services and push the remaining burden back on the county without public notice and the opportunity for all interested parties to rebid. The Mather project should have been publicly rebid with notice of those changes.

A review of the operating costs in the final changes to the RFP compared to the options that we proposed prior to canceling the existing Mather contract raised concerns. The contract that was offered was a 6-month contract for $772,500 designated to serve 140 clients in an employment program (which no providers bid on). The contract that was eventually awarded was a 6-month contract for $1.5 million ($3 million annually) to serve only 80 clients in a shelter. The new provider would be receiving $27,500 per client for shelter care annually. At that rate, the county would be incurring additional direct costs of $1,125,000 to provide services for the remaining 60 clients that would now be under their care. When you add those two numbers together, the cost to provide shelter services for 140 clients is $4,125,000 annually. Before the decision was made to cancel the existing Mather contract after 6 months, VOA had made the request to increase the annual funding by $1,000,000 from the then-current amount of $1,484,000 to $2,484,000 annually. That request was rejected; it was the amount needed together with other existing funding sources that would have kept the Mather employment program intact.

More Money for Fewer Services

This comparison is not being included to disparage local government personnel; it is another example of how federal funding can dictate program decisions in local social services. It is about losing local client services by being bound to bad federal policy. By changing the designation of Mather from transitional housing to a shelter, the program would qualify for Housing First funding because technically the county was "adding" shelter beds. The analysis here shows that more actual money will be spent despite removing critical services from the people who need them. This happens over and over again for the same reason. It is all taxpayers' money. It gets passed around through the same government agencies but with different guidelines based on where the policy originated. Most of the time, the public is treated as too naïve or stupid to see what is actually taking place in the trenches. There is no way to push back, unless some groups of concerned citizens just get pushed past their limit of tolerance in watching these failed policies do more harm than good. It is then that we should expect them to take steps that cause serious social agitation. We have seen this happen before in this country, several times and just recently.

Prior to the decision to terminate the contract at the end of 2019, the Mather employment program was also receiving funding that was worth up to $600,000 per year for workforce development through a federal program called SNAP (Supplemental Nutrition Assistance Program). The SNAP funding can only be used to pay for employment-related activities, so when the county canceled the VOA contract, which included employment-related activities, that funding was no longer available to provide training for unemployed homeless. This change of scope at Mather created a $600,000 loss to our community for employment training. Had the funding been increased for the employment contract to match what is being spent

149

at Mather today as a shelter, together with the SNAP funding, there would have been revenues of $4.6 million available: enough to continue the Mather Employment program, allowing robust employment and housing services to continue for 140 clients. That works out to $35,000 per client per year, which is higher than the level it had been operating for all of the fiscal years of 2014–2017. The decision to change the program to a shelter never considered the loss of the SNAP revenue and the additional benefits it would continue to bring to the region.

The SNAP funding for employment-related activities did not have an annual revenue cap at the time. There were literally tens of millions of dollars available to the State of California remaining through this program. The collaborative work done with the county on bringing those dollars to Sacramento had allowed us to increase revenues each year. Internally, Mather staff believed we could have qualified for up to $1 million through that program, annually, over the next 2 years. The termination of the employment contract eliminated that possibility.

The message from all of the county executives involved in the Mather discussion was the same. When asked about additional funding, they claimed the county did not have the funds needed to continue the existing programming at Mather. This is the same response that was received from four out of the five county supervisors. These supervisors were the same people who ended up approving the changes at Mather to fund it as a shelter. When you look at a financial comparison in actual dollars spent, the facts provide an interesting perspective. Whether it shows up on an individual ledger or not, the county is now committing at least $4,125,000 annually to provide shelter services for the new Mather population. Mather was staffed and ready to provide the full array of services for an employment program, with

20 years of history that showed many of the clients had been able to reduce barriers, receive training, find work and housing, and exit homelessness for good; and it could have been done for $1,500,000 less per year when measured in the public dollars that are now going to be expended at Mather each year for a shelter. "Tax users to tax payers" was the way our students' futures were referred to in the Mather employment program. Not anymore. It cannot be overstated: These decisions were driven by the funding availability at the time. The feds had money to spend, the county seemingly did not. The homeless needing this programming got the short straw.

When you compute the difference in real cost between a person who left the Mather program with a job and never returned to homelessness and a person who comes to a shelter program for a few months and is placed in permanent supportive housing, the numbers are shocking. A person leaving with employment, making as little as $15 per hour, is going to pay a minimum of $5,000 per year in taxes (sales taxes, income taxes, etc.) and no longer relies on other county services. The person placed in permanent supportive housing from a shelter program (based on costs reported in Orange County, California, in 2018) will cost the county close to $50,000 per year to support.[31] Over just a 10-year period, that costs a community at least $600,000 for each person. Now multiply that times seventy to a hundred people per year (the minimum number of people who were getting employment each year at Mather), and the financial impact is substantial. Had anyone thought to do a return-on-investment

31 Orange County United Way, "Homelessness in Orange County: The Costs to Our Community," https://www.unitedwayoc.org/wp-content/uploads/2017/03/Orange-County-Cost-Study-Homeless-Executive-Summary.pdf.

calculation to determine the best use of the Mather facilities comparing these models, the decisions should have changed. The other financial fact that was not considered was that a Mather graduate paying as little as $5,000 per year in income and sales taxes ends up paying back his or her own transitional housing program costs in 5 years. This never happens with permanent supportive housing solutions and rarely happens within the other Housing First models.

The additional cost to the community, based on these changes to the facility's use over 10 years, is well in excess of $40,000,000. It is the taxpayers who pick up that difference. That is a total worth mentioning. These increases do not take into consideration the additional cost to provide services for each unsheltered person living in the community. The number of people unsheltered can only grow when there are no programs that move people out of homelessness. The estimated cost for those homeless services (police, ambulance, emergency room, public health, navigators, cleanup, and all the county costs associated with homeless services) is well over $100,000 per person per year. This estimate was given to me in a meeting with the Sacramento County executive officer in 2018. The financial burden just gets harder to comprehend trying to apply this model to the growing homeless population.

The financial models presented here are based on historical outcomes from the Mather program. Most of that history happened before coordinated entry. During those years, the clients were selected by the referring service providers as being the most likely to succeed in the Mather program. It was a process of getting people ready to live independently, including financially, prior to moving into market housing. At one point, almost 70% of the students coming through the program were getting jobs and moving into market rate housing.[32] All of these people had been homeless and some chronically homeless in their recent past. At times, there were comments made from a few government officials that the Mather staff was "cherry picking" the clients. Those of us who worked at Mather know that was never the case. A system that moves people through steps of addressing needs, in an effort to prepare them for independent living, should not be confused with "cherry picking."

As a community, we have to work to find solutions to move as many people to self-sufficiency as possible. It is both the humane thing to work toward and by far the most financially sound alternative available. Inexplicably, that reasoning has been lost or distorted from view by the issues of funding availability. It is costing thousands of people the opportunity to improve their life now, with impacts that could last generations. That is an enormous price to pay for following funding and spending policy that denies opportunity for people to progress. This continues to happen every year at the federal, state, and community levels. What happened to the recently readopted motto for change in this country that says all Americans deserve equal opportunity? The homeless are not represented in this vision statement.

The move away from transitional housing with integrated supportive services has played out in communities all across the nation. Without this model, it is very difficult to see where the new stories of rebuilding broken lives and torn families will come from in the future within our homeless population. Redemption happens with structured opportunity, hard work, and a community that cares and steps in to help all of its citizens.

---

32 Our success rate with employment of our students fluctuated with the current economic conditions in the marketplace. When the job market was robust, our outcomes mirrored the market. During recessions and economic downturns, our results fluctuated downwards.

Operational Review and Review of Partnerships

This section is intended to provide a look behind the scenes of what is entailed in working in publicly funded social services (at least in California). We will share the things that worked well and reveal some of the really difficult issues that came up during the 10 years VOA was awarded the program management contract at Mather Campus. Included is information from some of the meetings with community decision-makers that were held prior to the eventual closure of the Mather programming. This information is intended to show how federal policy mandates can eliminate years of carefully constructed and effective programming put in place by local providers—people who understood the local issues and made adjustments over the years to address the needs.

Prior to 2010, Volunteers of America was awarded the contract to manage the homeless service program at Mather Campus. This was done through a traditional RFP process. The county made the decision that VOA was better suited to contract out and monitor the management of these programs than the county was. At that time, employment services remained subcontracted to Crossroads, and the family services were contracted to Next Move. There was a financial crisis in 2009, and an emergency-funding package was put together under the leadership of the county executives with the participation of the service providers.

In 2014, the operating budget for Mather was below break-even. This forced the need for cost-saving measures that included, first, the canceling of the contract with the employment service provider. At the time, the work being done by Crossroads was redundant with the work being done at the DHA One-Stop. The second cost-cutting move happened in 2015, after the additional funding reductions of $181,000 represented earlier in this chapter took place. This loss was mitigated by canceling the management contract of Next

Move. This was a very difficult move for both agencies. The actual program work that the Next Move team was doing on campus was excellent. The additional overhead and administrative costs were where the savings were realized. VOA was able to retain all but one of their operational employees. Many of them stayed through the closings of the programs.

VOA had contracted directly with Sacramento County, and they were responsible for monitoring the operation. VOA was assigned a program monitor. The monitor oversaw the operational performance and outcomes of the programs and was responsible for the file and operational audits. *That relationship with the county, early on, became a solid partnership that kept the mutual interests of the students as its top priority.* There were a few disagreements about funding and operations along the way, but they were constructive and supportive. The positive outcomes and the results during that period reflected a strong partnership.

In 2016, the county contracted the job of managing the HUD funds coming into Sacramento to a new agency. That agency became the contract monitor for the Mather programs. In April of 2016, they sent an internal auditor out to perform a file audit. This auditor would end up also becoming the program monitor. She made her first trip to Mather on Good Friday in 2016. It was obvious from the first hour she was there that this was going to be a contentious relationship. She accused staff of making serious financial errors on client fees. It is very difficult to speculate exactly what the motivation was for this particular individual, but her actions significantly set back the program financially and operationally, as detailed below. Her interpretation of HUD policy and a desire to maintain strict adherence created more harm than good.

We were instructed by this monitor to go back through every file, for 3 years, and create a separate general ledger for each file that included all the financial transactions for the term of each student's stay. We had to create a new full-time position to take on this additional work. It took a little over 1 year to finish creating the general ledgers. After it was completed, we were directed to deliver all of those files (dozens of boxes) to the agency's office for review. The message being sent was that students had been overcharged with fees and rent during their stay and VOA was going to be required to pay it back to them. Our own review of these ledgers, when they were completed, showed that we had undercharged on a few occasions but that there was no evidence of overcharging. The files were delivered in late 2017 for their review. The program closed in December of 2019 and we never heard another word regarding those files. We have to assume that our accounting was accurate and fair. The cost to recreate those ledgers was well over $50,000.

Over the ensuing 12 months, this individual continued to challenge fee structures and targeted the mandatory food stamp program that had been in place since the program started in 1998. With support from the San Francisco HUD office, the mandatory food program was determined to be in violation of existing HUD policy. Research showed that the team that founded the Mather program had received an exception from that policy at the beginning of the program. It was noted in the original file that the exception required additional approval after a trial period. The county had never followed up with obtaining the additional approvals, so that part of the program was forcibly removed. The payment for meals became voluntary, and VOA was forced to incur the costs of installing refrigerators and microwaves in the common areas for people who chose to prepare their own meals. The county had originally established the food stamp program for two reasons. The first was that it was to be a part of the programming that taught basic financial skills and management of resources. The second was that it created the extra revenue needed to pay for the food service, including operating a commercial kitchen and providing three hot meals per day for all the single students.

The history of the food program and collecting food stamp fees will show that the federal Supplemental Nutrition Assistance Program office had approved it before Mather opened. Regardless, the monitor lobbied with the HUD regional office that the program had only been given the right to collect the food stamps during a trial period as part of a pilot program. Since it had not been reapproved, it was deemed no longer valid. The regional office upheld that ruling and the program lost a large portion of the food fees. The refrigerators and microwaves were installed. After 6 months, we had refrigerators full of rotting food and microwave ovens that were getting no use. The larger negative impact to the program was that many of the newer students were selling their food stamps to buy alcohol and drugs. This was another case of federal government intervention that added substantial costs and produced negative results. We have interviewed hundreds of Mather alumni who successfully finished this program; every individual we asked told us that the food stamp program and kitchen experience were a key to their overall success. They all may not have liked contributing their food stamps every month, but given the time to reflect on the program's importance, they have been unanimous in their support.

That program monitor left that agency, and the county made the decision to take back the program monitoring in 2018. The food stamp program was reinstated for a few months and then revoked again. In the meantime, we had lobbied hard to have the food service be an included part of the program, at no cost to the students, with the food costs covered in the county contract. The county was not willing to increase the funding, so a monthly fee-based meal program was created that was voluntary. Interestingly, now that the county has turned the singles program into a 3-month shelter with a new provider, their contract amount includes covering the cost of food service. Still another example of how the source of funding can influence programming.

Alcohol and Drug Use and Homeless Services

The policy shifts that impact homeless services in relation to substance abuse and addiction have been extremely difficult to comprehend. Let's start with the early history of Housing First. In 1992, Dr. Sam Tsemberis, a faculty member of the Department of Psychiatry of the New York School Medicine, founded Pathways to Housing in New York City. It was based on the belief that housing is a basic human right that should not be denied to anyone, even those abusing alcohol and other substances.[33] This philosophy was adopted by HUD and is now an established practice in their Housing First models.[34]

Research would indicate that the Housing First program models that were initially developed had some critical differences in their make-up and operation than the rapid rehousing programs we are seeing today. I feel the most obvious difference can be found in the "wrap-around" services. The earliest models called for "intense wrap around services," particularly during the first few months. Many of the current rapid rehousing programs provide only "light touch" case management. Chronically homeless people with addictions need substantial support to overcome the issues of addiction while maintaining their own household. Transitional housing programs created a "therapeutic community" design, which allows individuals

33 Pathways Housing First website, https://www.pathwayshousingfirst.org

34 United States Interagency Council on Homelessness, "Housing First Checklist: Assessing Projects and Systems for a Housing First Orientation," September 28, 2016, https://www.usich.gov/tools-for-action/housing-first-checklist/

to support each other in recovery while working through the other program components. SAMSHA (Substance Abuse and Mental Health Agency) is a federal agency that is tasked with providing information on substance abuse and mental health treatment. When HUD was funding transitional housing, SAMSHA and NIH (National Institutes of Health Institute on Drug Abuse) published a number of materials on the benefit of therapeutic community design.[35] Since the reduction in transitional housing support from HUD, there do not seem to be places that would accommodate the establishment of a therapeutic community design component.

Whatever the reasons behind the policy shift, a very slippery slope has been created. It seems like there are not enough people (who are not alcohol or drug addicts) who know the truth about this disease. *And it is a disease*, one that causes permanent restructuring of brain cells and can cause significant behavioral changes. In many cases, addiction can cause severe mental health conditions that are extremely difficult to overcome. For those who need more information, here are two excellent sources recommended for reading:

1. The book *Addiction, Why Can't They Just Stop?*[36]

2. The 2016 Surgeon General's report, *Facing Addiction in America.*[37]

---

35 National Institute on Drug Abuse, "What Is a Therapeutic Community's Approach?" Therapeutic Communities Research Report, July 2015, https://www.drugabuse.gov/publications/research-reports/therapeutic-communities/what-therapeutic-communitys-approach

36 John Hoffman and Susan Froemke, *Addiction: Why Can't They Just Stop?* (New York: Rodale, 2007).

37 U.S. Department of Health and Human Services (HHS), Office of the Surgeon General, *Facing Addiction in America: The Surgeon General's Report on Alcohol, Drugs, and Health* (Washington, DC: HHS, November 2016).

There are two absolute truths regarding the chronically homeless: (1) After a significant time on the street, an individual will have developed a drug or alcohol problem that will most likely become an addiction. (2) If this addiction is not treated, it will interfere with the individual's ability to live independently. A 20-year history of serving the homeless at Mather shows that 80% or more of the population, year in and year out, were struggling with addictions.

How does it make sense to take the most vulnerable (guaranteed to have a substance abuse problem that is most likely an addiction) and put them in an independent living arrangement with no requirements to get treatment? We have had experience with hundreds of people who have worked their way through an addiction and have gone on to lead a productive life in their community. Every one of them has said that getting sober and staying sober was critical to their success. On the issues of basic human rights, we believe that every human being has the basic right to have a chance to lead a productive and inclusive life in his or her community. There are some who will need and deserve multiple chances to achieve this goal. It is a very difficult physical and psychological hurdle to overcome addiction on the first try. *In the long run, all of us benefit through each person's success and we all pay for each life that is abandoned.*

At Mather we battled with the contracted monitoring agency for a few years over the right and need to do drug testing. A major element of our argument to do drug testing included the benefits to our students that came from maintaining a clean and sober environment. In fairness to the monitoring agency personnel, having requirements to drug testing were and still remain against "the rules" of HUD's Housing First mandates. It was frustrating at Mather to be forced into having to use coordinated entry and to be bound by the other Housing First rules, even after Mather had stopped receiving HUD funds. Especially considering that the majority of the students were in strong favor of drug testing. The students, who were striving to succeed, knew that having widespread use on campus created an ever-present trigger to start using again for anyone in recovery.

For 12 months during 2017–2018, we were ordered to suspend any regular drug testing. This meant that there were no sobriety requirements for admission, and only intervention-based testing based on abnormal behavior for existing students. During that period, the percentage of clients who were actively using (that we were aware of) climbed over 40% and impacted 64 of the 140 students. This kind of excessive activity brought with it drug dealing, prostitution, theft, and violence. We had it all at Mather for a period. It took the help of concerned managers with the alcohol and drug treatment side of county operations (who were operating a clean and sober family program at Mather) to force the return of drug testing to all residents in the community. Once that was back in place, it took just 3 months to restore order. It was a very difficult time for both students and the staff, and it cost several of the clients their opportunity to finish the program. Even though it was difficult, it reinforced our position that sobriety was foundational to the continued success of our students in achieving their goal of becoming independent.

Reinstatement of drug testing was a positive change for the students who were trying hard to finish the program. During the ongoing debates on drug testing, the question had been asked on at least two occasions by two public officials responsible for homeless services: "Can't people work during the day or the week and then have a few beers or a little marijuana during their time off?" Our answer was basically this: There are plenty of people in the world who can do that, but those people do not end up chronically homeless and at Mather Campus. The fact that this question was asked at all was revealing. People who had sat in on Mather client interviews would understand that the majority of our clients struggled with addiction for years and had dealt with multiple relapses along the way. These people could not be near the substances, let alone be involved in casual use. For them, casual use would result in a short path back to full-blown addiction.

That is, unfortunately, the norm for drug and alcohol addiction. The triggers (the impulse to drink or use) are very real and extremely powerful. The biggest trigger of all is having access to substances. Hearing those questions raised concerns that the people who were managing the implementation of policy for homeless services could not relate to the clients' needs. There seemed to be a lack of understanding about the ravages of alcohol and drug addictions, including how very difficult it is to stop. The physiological need to use for an addict often overrides other important decision-making needs, even the basic decisions that have to be made to maintain good health, financial security, and family ties. Addiction is a mean and pervasive disease.

The Final Stages of the Program Deconstruction

While these issues regarding alcohol and drug testing were taking place, there were public funding changes impacting the Mather program that were highlighted earlier in this chapter. Looking at the financial timeline provided earlier, by the beginning of 2017, the program had lost $380,000 in public funding from the prior 3 years. Some of that loss was bridged with private fundraising and the reserves from the local affiliate of Volunteers of America. By October of 2017, it was official that Mather was not going to continue to receive federal funding for the singles transitional housing program from HUD. That change, by itself, would create a $2.5 million deficit. HUD funds at Mather had accounted for over 50% of the public funding coming into this program. Knowing that the loss of these funds was inevitable, we made an initial application for SNAP funding, which was believed, over time, could make up $1 million of that loss. It was becoming clear in 2016 that Mather was going to lose HUD funding for the singles program in the next few years. However, we anticipated that Mather would have until October of 2019 to replace this funding. That was based on the fact that HUD had extended the timeline for local Continuums of Care (COCs) to submit Notice of Funds Availability (NOFA) applications that included transitional housing programs through October 2017. Had an application been submitted to include Mather at that time, funding would have continued to include the period of October 2018 through September 2019.

This timing is a little confusing, but basically the HUD funding applications, when approved, funded programs starting 1 year from the application date through the end of the following federal funding year. VOA had completed the application submission and attended the COC meeting where the vote was going to take place on whether to let Mather apply for a final 12 months. A councilman from the City of Sacramento came to that meeting to speak on behalf of VOA and the Mather program. Everyone knew that HUD funding for transitional housing was going to end soon. The pitch that was made included disclosure that we would need to find funding alternatives over the next few years to maintain the Mather employment program. Also, that extra time was needed to locate enough revenue to cover the loss of those HUD funds. The program was still the only program in Sacramento County that was providing job training and employment for homeless single adults and a true path to self-sufficiency. Interestingly, many of those who were representing providers in the room had depended on Mather for years as the place to move their clients to a higher level of care. The councilman followed up our presentation by giving an impassioned pitch for the important work being done at Mather and how vital it was to the community.

In the end, the COC board voted not to include Mather in that NOFA application. It is unclear if they were concerned about completely losing the $3.5 million dollars of HUD funding that had been coming to Sacramento through Mather or were looking to increase funding for newer programs. Most likely, the decision included motivations for both of those goals. This is another case of a funding source and their use restrictions dictating decisions that might not include the best interests of those they were intended to benefit.

This refusal to include the Mather Singles program in the NOFA application was a financial gut punch. It officially put VOA and the Mather staff in a desperate scramble to save, what we felt, was still the most comprehensive and financially responsible program for homeless services in the county. The first reaction was to sit down with the Sacramento County representatives who had oversight for the operation of Mather and make the request to help find additional funding. To be fair, there had been public meetings held requesting changes to the county general fund budget that included an increase in funding of $1 million for Mather the year before.

Unfortunately, that only covered a portion of the deficit. Shortly after receiving that increase, the state ruled that Mather no longer qualified for a $165,000 annual CalWorks grant that had been in place for years. VOA also lost the right to collect rental payments from a separate program that had located to the campus several years prior. It appears this ruling also came from the state. Both of those funding sources had been a part of the county-approved 2010 emergency funding package for Mather. These decisions resulted in another $237,000 annual reduction. Then there was the elimination of the mandatory food stamp collection requirement that further reduced revenue to the program by $150,000. Even including the $1 million general fund increase, with the loss of HUD funding and these other reductions, the Mather program annual revenue would be reduced by $1.4 million in 2018. It was the unofficial end of that program as we knew it.

The Failed Media Campaign

All future requests for additional funding support were met with the answer "The county has no additional funds," or more succinctly, "There isn't any more money." It was clear that there were not going to be public funds made available through traditional lines. VOA made the decision to create a media campaign to target community support for keeping this program open. It was to be an attempt to attract financial support from multiple sources. We hoped to create private support as well as support from the county to find the public funding needed to keep the program operating. After all, these facilities had been provided to the county from the Air Force to be used only for homeless services. The only decision remaining was what services would be provided. This attempt to keep the employment program alive was made because it had operated as the "gold standard" for homeless services for 20 years in our region. And a similar media strategy had saved the program in 2010.

It was to be a reminder that there were 140 apartments, a fully operational commercial kitchen, classrooms, and a dedicated DHA One-Stop all in place. All were molded and linked together to operate an employment to housing program. The facilities would remain restricted by the regulatory agreement to be used exclusively for homeless services for another 20 years. The program had won two national awards for excellence. There should have been an all-out effort to keep it operating, so a public appeal was made, which included local news and press coverage. Past program graduates were enlisted to come in and tell their story as part of a video campaign. Maybe the biggest motivating factor for all of us working there was the realization that once this service model was disassembled, it would be next to impossible to reconstruct it at any time in the near future, if ever.

There were meetings scheduled with each of the county supervisors to talk about the financial issues and the pending loss of the program. Each one of them professed sympathy and love for the program but re-echoed the sentiment that the county just did not have any more money. We pointed out that in a meeting with the County Executive a few months earlier, we had learned the cost to the county to provide homeless services to care for and monitor the homeless is over $100,000 per year per person (and he said that was a conservative estimate). The argument that we were trying to present to the supervisors was that the program cost per person was far less at Mather ($26,000 per person per year) than it was to provide services to them on the street. Plus, there was the extra benefit that many of the Mather clients became employed, exiting homelessness and becoming tax-paying citizens. The vocal support that we received in those meetings from the county supervisors did not lead to the hoped-for results.

There is little doubt that the Sacramento County staff and the Board of Supervisors were looking at a very difficult financial situation at that time, with projections that only got worse for the next few years, and that was before the pandemic. This is not an accusation that anyone was being misleading about the county budget. We realize there are many services to pay for, and each one has to be reviewed in a number of ways; for example, what services have to be funded and which agency within the county is responsible. I have great respect for each of the supervisors and the work they have done. Still, there are unanswered questions about the unopposed closing of the Mather employment program and its replacement by a shelter. (It may have been part of the attempt to align the Mather housing units with future Housing First funding streams.) Regardless, the actions taken to date, with respect to the use of those Mather facilities, are costing more to support the current population than was the pre-existing employment program. This is despite the loss of a significant number of services and benefits to the homeless people in the county.

The operational changes now in place were aimed at qualifying Mather services for future federal and state funding streams. That does not obscure the fact that hundreds of hours of critical service opportunities were erased from the homeless population, hundreds of thousands of dollars in other federal funds restricted to "employment-related activities" were lost to our community (SNAP funds), and tens of thousands of dollars in private support for the employment program are no longer paying dividends. Giving credence to the complexity of county services and the county budgets doesn't change the fact that the annual county budget is $4.4 billion (county fiscal year 2019–2020, per their website). The general fund portion of their budget (discretionary spending) is $1.8 billion for this period. The $1 million in additional funds that were requested for Mather would have kept the employment program operating, and $1.5 million would have kept the services up to date and robust. That is 0.034% of the 2019–2020 general fund budget.

It would have been helpful to have constructive conversations about the perceived impact of the media campaign with the county staff while it was being aired. Certain individuals at the county felt they were being accused of letting the program close, according to some of the feedback we received. There are two sides to every story, and if there was negative perception within the county that has to be taken as legitimate. Unfortunately, unlike the reception for a very similar media campaign in 2010, which was perceived as leading to a mutual benefit, this one was not. Not only did the campaign fail, it seems to have triggered unintended consequences that caused damage at VOA. The campaign was focused on the great work that had been done at Mather and what was about to be lost to the community.

There was additional feedback that a few of the county staff felt they had not been given credit for the program successes over the years. It is difficult to discount another's perception, but a closer look at what actually took place each year raises serious questions about this view. The collaborative success at Mather was promoted year after year at the Mather graduations. County officials, the DHA staff, and the board supervisors were highlighted as integral partners. In retrospect, very few of the county staff who were invited actually attended Mather graduations, which might explain their response. Also, every spring, dating back to 2005, VOA held an annual fundraising breakfast, an event that was attended by over 400 community leaders and county officials. This was another public gathering where our successful partnership with the county at Mather was fully recognized. There were also brochures handed out to all who visited Mather that put the county at the top of the list of contributing partners.

By 2018, VOA was operating the singles program on 57% of the revenues that were coming into Mather back in 2014. When the contract year of 2019 began in July of 2018, it was only 52% of the 2014 funding. In addition, the county had removed four full-time employees from their One-Stop office at Mather. This caused a serious workforce shortage in the program, as existing VOA staff were forced to pick up the 160 hours per week that were lost when those county employees left. During the years that the funding sources were being reduced and county staff were being removed, there were never any corresponding reductions to the required client services in the contract; the opposite actually took place. The new program monitor assigned by the county in 2018 made additional demands for information, paperwork, and meetings. She constantly clashed with the staff over process and procedures and management of clients. The stress and energy drain caused by the increase in work and reduction in revenue on Mather staff was huge. It was all wasted energy, especially considering that the decision had probably already been made to convert Mather to a shelter.

The issues at Mather came to a head in early 2019. There would be no additional public funding coming into Mather. Volunteers of America could no longer provide the services outlined in the con-tract. The board of directors of VOA informed the executive staff that they could no longer subsidize the losses at Mather. The pro-gram that had been the most treasured at VOA for over a decade for the work done there and the lives that had been changed, was going to close. The county requested a summary of services VOA could continue to provide, with their financial contribution being capped at $1,455,000 annually. VOA replied that they could no longer pro-vide a full-service employment to housing program. At that point, the county reduced the existing 2020 contract with VOA from 1 year to 6 months and put the singles program out to bid. Earlier in this chapter, we chronicled how that ended up; with a very unusual (possibly unethical) public bid process. It is hard not to feel like the transfer of services had been preplanned out of the public eye.

For the last 3 years, business relations with the homeless ser-vices division of Sacramento County have been difficult. These are my personal observations; they make the rules, control the funding, monitor the performance, and along the way change scope and process as they see fit. Too much resistance puts the contractor at risk for loss of work. Continued attempts to question the methods or demands will likely lead to the loss of more opportunity. The Mather staff had an excellent relationship with the County One-Stop staff prior to the policy changes that chased off five of their six staff. The entire staff at the DHA One-Stop supported the media campaign (they are all gone now). Over the following 2 years, after the media campaign had run its course, the relationship with the county's managers has noticeably changed. My view (and it is mine alone) is that there has been a focused effort to replace VOA on all of the county contracts for programs where they were providing homeless services. There is no option for recourse when situations like this happen with government agencies. All the power, money, and direction are fully controlled on that side of the ledger and out of the public view.

I find it disheartening that Volunteers of America, the organization that has been serving the homeless along with other disenfranchised populations in Sacramento since 1911 (109 years) was impacted so hard for reasons yet to be explained. VOA has served tens of thousands in this community over the years and has been a willing partner in many emergency service programs with the county, often with minimal notice and often with a promise that a contract would be in place when the work was started. The closing of the Mather program resulted in having to lay off or reassign more than 50 people who were the employment program. They taught life skills classes and recovery classes, and they provided pre-employment training. The curriculum that was developed and updated for those classes was remarkable and filled an 8-inch-thick binder. They created individual service and employment plans for people. They managed the students' community service work and vocational training needs, and put them in front of employers who would eventually hire them. As I write this, all of that is gone. The biggest loss is the intellectual capital that left with the people who did the work. Some may think it is a small thing to recreate, rehire, and reorganize all of those things into another cost-effective and mission-effective system. Think again.

CHAPTER 12

What Now?

I NEED TO PROVIDE A SHORT DISCLAIMER REGARDING THIS chapter. It is centered on my experience and views of the events surrounding homeless care, much of which has already been covered. My views are shared by many who have been trying to provide decent services for the homeless, but I don't know how to avoid overuse of the pronoun "I" for the next few paragraphs. So here we go: From where I sit, the state of California is in trouble. My guess is, the same issues show up in many of the states in our union; I just happen to live here and work here. You might feel the need for more information about me to make a better judgment on my reliability to assess the issues, make judgments, and propose new ideas. I have included a detailed biography, written specifically to provide some background, on where and how my opinions were formulated. You can find it immediately after the epilogue.

My question is: How do we start the conversation about changes that could lead to better futures for the homeless and the communities they/we live in? There are no quick fixes at this point.

Imagination and hard work need to be included over the next 20 years to carve out a better future. We have to look beyond short-term plans proposed by local politicians every election cycle. Those plans have chased funding options and have neglected to challenge many of the critical services that have been removed. We are experiencing the consequences of that neglect. The new solutions have to be broader than just housing units. They have to include improving the prospects of the people. We have ignored that calling for 200 years in our prison systems. We have not had effective rehabilitation programs for people who we know we have to reintegrate back into our communities. Most prisoners who are released commit crimes again. Ignoring the rehabilitation of the homeless population, whom we are contemplating storing in subpar housing solutions, is destined to have the same result: More people in the system who are no better off than when we started "serving" them.

Similarities with State Prison System

Problems of the homeless and the lack of progress on reducing their numbers have a lot of similarities to the state prison system here in California. According to the California Department of Corrections report from 2016, back in 2013 the federal government had given the state a mandate to reduce their prison population to 137.5% of capacity from what was then around 145% of capacity by January of 2016. Ultimately, they were given a 2-year extension. There was also a mandate that the 9,500 prisoners who were being held out of state be returned to California. The report went on to say that they would not meet those goals in 2016. There was a lot of filler in the report but no clear-cut plan addressing the overcrowding issue. In the last few years, several state assembly bills aimed at reducing the prison population were passed. AB 109 allowed prisons to move the "lower-level" criminals to local county jails as a way to lower the prison numbers. That was followed a few years later by early release plans, including the latest one meant to reduce the chance of COVID-19 spreading in the jails. Governor Newsom just signed twenty-five new bills for criminal justice reform. One of those expunges criminal records the day the prisoner is released. Another increases benefits for victims of crime, and still another eliminates sentence enhancement for criminals who committed the same crime a second or third time. There's also one that reduces prison time for those prisoners who voluntarily participate in rehabilitation programs.

When you look at the policy changes that have come about, intentionally or not, through Housing First for the homeless and compare them with the constant policy changes in the California prison system, what should jump out at you is the failure to deal with the root causes of their problems. In homelessness, there is now a rush to get people off of the street and store them in housing options that don't include support for the underlying issues that lead to homelessness in the first place. In the prison system, there is more emphasis on reduced sentencing and creating early releases (with enhanced payoff to victims), instead of seriously ramping up rehabilitation efforts. True prison reform would deal with the deplorable conditions and overall treatment of people you know are going to be released back into the community.

The current combined deficiencies in the rehabilitation efforts of the Department of Corrections and the various homeless services programs will provide a steady new inflow of homeless into the community for the foreseeable future. It will happen as a result of the continuous recycle of the existing homeless who are being rehoused without resolution of their underlying issues. Then there is the new influx of prisoners being released from local jails, who have not been prepared to function in the world they are returning to in their community. By example, a criminal held in a local jail has to make only six to eight decisions a day, because there is nothing to do in a local jail. At least in the state prisons, there is a yard to walk in, a library to find books to read, and different jobs to fill the time. Upon release from a local jail, a person will be faced with ten times as many decisions each day, and the stress has proven to be overwhelming.

There are several excellent private rehabilitation efforts happening in prisons in California that are doing excellent work. What is lacking is a statewide commitment to provide rehabilitation for the total population. Additionally, moving the population from prisons to local jails for 1 to 2 years prior to release has the capacity to undo any prior rehab work.

There are additional factors that will impact the number of homeless in our community in the next year as a result of COVID-19 restrictions in California. Unemployment and small business closures are ramping up, and the impacts are being held at bay by stimulus checks. There are also COVID-19 restrictions on evictions for nonpayment of rent and similar restrictions on foreclosures for nonpayment of mortgages. It is very difficult to speculate on how these issues will ultimately impact the numbers when the subsidies stop.

We have looked at the new housing options that are being discussed for the homeless. You can make up your own mind on the viability of those being effective long-term solutions. Personally, I am extremely concerned about the long-term impacts of these extremely shortsighted decisions. It feels like it is time to sound an alarm bell. We could be looking at unprecedented numbers of homeless in this state over the next few years, with huge state budget deficits based on current circumstances. I am sure everyone has heard the definition

of insanity: doing the same thing over and over and expecting different results. It is time to embrace significant change. The good news
with the homeless issues is that we have pieces that we know work
for segments of this population. We need to reconfigure the puzzle
and rethink the long-term impacts of what we are doing.

How Do We Move Forward from Here?

It is time we find leaders who look beyond their next election cycle
and have the fortitude to develop intelligent long-term solutions.
We need leaders who are capable of developing collaborations that
cross some old established lines. How do we create an environment
that explores more fundamental change? Of course, these actions
depend on what kind of community and/or country we ultimately
want. In searching for answers, we have to make this as nonpolitical
as possible—otherwise we automatically lose 45% of everyone. And
we need input from everyone who wants to see real constructive
change—change that truly represents equitable opportunity for all,
that can find its way permanently into the fabric of this country.

I believe we can take a big step in that direction by properly
addressing the homeless situation with truly long-term benevolent
planning for this population; we have to start somewhere. There
are some ideas presented over the next few pages that could be pur-
sued to help realign the direction of homeless services. We have to
start with the understanding that change is very difficult. It is not
so difficult in the execution of the parts, but experience has taught
us that the politics tied to constructive change is a formidable road-
block. It is going to take a monumental push from the ground up
(concerned citizens and business owners alike) to push back against
the forces that have seized control of the current system and their
assets (which are not infinite). Before we lay out potential new

ideas, let's look at another example of how politics can undermine constructive planning.

Avoiding Politics and Missed Opportunities

In 2018, Mather needed additional funding to continue operating as an employment to housing program for the homeless. By this time, we had exhausted discussions with the county personnel and the board of supervisors to help find that funding through county agencies. At the same time, the City of Sacramento was facing a crisis with the downtown business partnership and their concerns regarding the homeless downtown. There were growing complaints from those business owners about the homeless sleeping in their storefront doorways, defecating and urinating on their property, leaving used needles there, and panhandling the customers. The problem had been growing for some time; it had become a real problem for these businesses, and it was becoming a real problem for the mayor and his team. What ultimately became the frontline solution to this particular problem and the associated political pressure was the decision to renovate a downtown hotel, specifically to create shelter beds for the group of homeless people sleeping in the storefronts and surrounding areas. It was a $13 million solution to accommodate approximately one hundred people for around 18 months. After that, the hotel would be converted to permanent supportive housing. The program included the additional expense of finding scattered site permanent supportive housing solutions for those being moved into the hotel over the ensuing 18 months.

It took over 1 year from the time the decision was made to convert the hotel until the property could actually house clients. This was because of the massive improvements that were required to pass the building and safety codes. Prior to the reconstruction of the hotel, we had approached both the downtown partnership and the City of Sacramento with a proposal that we would take a minimum of one hundred homeless people out of the City of Sacramento shelters every year and enroll them in the Mather program. This would allow them to relocate those who were homeless downtown into their other shelter locations in the city. Our offer was to do this for $1 million of funding each year. We had enthusiastic interest from one city councilman, who got us a presentation with a city manager who was non-engaging, to say the least. Eventually, we were granted a meeting with the mayor. At the beginning of that meeting, he told us he would give us 15 minutes, basically dismissing any further discussion.

He did say that the funding stream that would be needed to utilize Mather as a solution had restrictions that required adding *new* housing units to their inventory, and therefore Mather did not qualify. I have since learned that this is a restriction, but that there were several ways to reclassify existing housing units to qualify. Also, the local government has some authority to innovate. In subsequent conversations with the county supervisors, I learned that there were grave concerns between the county and the city about who would ultimately retain control over use of the Mather housing units that might be unworkable, based on their history with each other. Obviously, the proposal went nowhere.

Let's talk about the missed opportunity. The first missed opportunity was for the program to stay open with no additional cost to the county. Mather could have taken almost all of the first one hundred clients well ahead of the opening of the hotel, which would have opened up other city shelter space to move people off of the downtown streets much faster. If the decision had been made to renovate the hotel anyway for future permanent supportive housing, the interim use would have been in addition to the Mather assistance. The hotel renovation should have been reconsidered as a temporary homeless project anyway, based on the high cost, limited use, and the concerns around the overall quality and safety of the structure.

A pure cost comparison of the solution that utilized Mather beds versus the hotel reconstruction should raise real concerns about how decisions are being made. For $13 million, we could have served close to one thousand homeless shelter clients over the next 10 years, with the real possibility that well over half could have left homelessness for good with employment and housing. Even if the decision to convert that hotel into permanent supportive housing makes financial sense on its own merits, a chance was missed to give more than five hundred people an opportunity to obtain the tools needed to end their homeless cycle. If we compute the additional cost to the community on losing those chances, we are talking millions of dollars again. This is exactly the kind of political decision-making that cripples our ability to work our way through tough issues. Again, five hundred people were denied the chance to change their life; how is that not discrimination at its worst? This bad "no-decision" to utilize Mather was the result of a political power dispute with little or no thought regarding the missed opportunity for these citizens. This is just one sequence of events, at one point in time, in one county, in one state.

We started by commenting on the problems with the top-down approach that happens with government control, and the problems with virtually every important policymaking decision that it produces. We attempted to show the lack of knowledge about who makes up the homeless population, and more importantly, their potential. Now policy-makers are trying to downplay the impacts of substance abuse and co-occurring mental health under a brand-new use of the term "harm reduction." Yet we continue down this path of following the one-size-fits-all policy that is the product of our federal government. People are going to have to demand change to those practices if we are to have any chance to be a nation that truly cares for each other.

Broader objectives might also include looking to see if there are savings that could be reallocated toward other public service needs. There should be a complete operational and financial audit of all of the service departments in each county that reviews their operating policies and budgets with the same objectives in mind. Is there room to reduce and reallocate funds? Returning to the fact that it costs our county an estimated $100,000 per person per year to provide services to the homeless in this county (with no progress to show for 10 years) should signal an obvious opportunity to do a complete audit. Initiatives like this would require significant work and cultural shifts, but could provide significant benefits to taxpayers and citizens. Simply staying the current course is not working; we are already in trouble with the size of the homeless problem. It is not just policy-makers and social service providers who are seeing the growth; today, virtually everyone is aware and concerned about the growing problem of homelessness.

I do not claim to have all of the answers; I never have and I never will. Therefore, I hope to see a process that assembles a representative group of concerned citizens and service providers—people who would be willing to gather to assimilate all the relevant information needed to collectively rebuild a system that has the comprehensive care and services in place to dramatically improve our results. The first draft of an ideal system of care should be devoid of budget constraints and any current built-in funding biases. What does the best system look like? How close can we get with the resources available today? What can we do in the next 5 years to move toward having the best system of national care in our own community? What does a public audit of current government spending on community services show that might be reallocated to a system of care?

Let's review this statement from HUD on the Housing First model: "Our goal is to end homelessness, not substance abuse." We have so much hard data that suggest substance abuse (particularly when it leads to addiction) is a major contributor to homelessness and very often leads to mental health issues. This issue has to be addressed for anyone hoping to re-enter the workforce and maintain a healthy lifestyle. It should also be addressed for families with children. If HUD is opting out, each community has to find a way to opt in on this topic.

Putting a System in Motion

We need a place where we can start to match services with the needs of our homeless citizens. Ultimately, we need a bigger, more comprehensive evaluation and approach, but we can institute some positive changes in the interim. That can happen with a thorough review of the programs and services that are remaining in the community. A current directory of services should be produced that not only categorizes services available and provides information on capacity, including whether it is private pay, publicly funded, or both. It should also include contact names and numbers. A series of provider meetings should be held to augment the group that is having the initial discussions on resetting the system of care. We need to understand how the need for their services aligns with their current capacity.

There are a number of programs in place that could serve as a place to start reconstructing the current system of care into something that, in time, provides more diverse opportunities for the homeless. Immediate goals would include planning designed to improve service utilization by aligning the resources available with the needs of the population. These actions would require some pushback against the one-size-fits-all federal policy that is at the core of the HUD funding requirements. The biggest hurdle in pursuing this objective will come from the officials and providers that have tied all of their future planning around the Housing First restrictions. There could be an opportunity to request funding for a new mixed model of care, but it would require total buy-in and support from the local COC.

The following outline contains important elements that are either missing or not connected in a coordinated system of care for the homeless today. The optimum word in the last sentence is *care*; it was the motivation for this book. Moving to this system would require adding services and rebuilding missing elements. It is not a detailed plan but an outline for a fluid system that allows people to progress. Of course, there is a need for efficiency and cost-effective services. Having said that, if you were to do a historical inspection of *any organization* that provides services or products to people, you will find that those who put all of their effort into cost effectiveness, at the expense of customer service, usually failed at their mission. What has transpired, over the past few years, is a continual reduction in the services that address the quality of life for large segments of the homeless population. The move away from treating the issues that lead people to become homeless is in opposition to efforts to provide trauma-informed care.

Let's start with a hypothetical outline of the components needed to begin rebuilding a system of *care* for the homeless.

1. A local review and revision of the definition of "homeless" to more effectively capture the depth of the population. Completed by the local COC, this would be designed to

both understand the total scope of the population as well as separate those who are homeless but do not qualify for HUD-funded programs.

2. Keep and revise the coordinated entry system.

    a. Navigators would still register and test all homeless residents.

    b. Initial temporary housing placement would always include a shelter option, assuming availability.

    c. Scoring would be revised to test for specific placement options based on needs. The most vulnerable would stay at the top of the list for permanent supportive housing and shelter options.

    d. Final review of test scores and triaging (for placement) would be completed by a panel of professionals that includes medical and mental health specialists.

    e. Homeless Management Information System would be updated to identify the number of open beds on any given day in all participating programs.

3. Placement opportunities would include the following:

    a. Shelters for families or individuals (open for all homeless): Preferred stay up to 90 days, limited options to extend. Shelter options would be open to individuals prior to triage if necessary. All other placement options below would require triaging and a referral first. Triaging could and should happen in the shelters.

b. Housing First options remain the first option for clients with minimum barriers. Also consider adding significant accessible services to these programs.

c. Increase the number of residential alcohol and drug recovery programs (3 to 6 months).

d. Increase the number of mental health workers and their ability to work with the homeless.

e. Residential employment to housing programs with integrated services (month-to-month stay of 18 to 24 months). Permanent locations for these programs are preferred, but other options could be investigated. There could be adjunct options added to existing plans for Tiny Home programs, tent cities, and the idea of using parking lots for temporary housing in cars.

4. Permanent supportive housing (individuals with severe physical or mental health disabilities).

5. Strategically placed satellite employment readiness and placement programs publicly funded; transportation included.

6. Develop and implement physical health programs that include recreational options for singles and family members.

There are hotlines (211) and navigators continuing to populate the coordinated entry list that exists today with hundreds of homeless people in the system. There is also a fully populated Homeless Management Information System that is designed to show where each individual who has been registered is currently residing. We should start by looking at some of the areas that are creating blind spots in the program. At some point, we have to build into our system a way to track those who are actually homeless but do not fit the definition needed to receive federal or state assistance. At the front of the system, we need effective triaging that could actually develop a phase-one Individual Service Plan that makes preliminary recommendations on the services that are needed for each individual and includes information on the goals of the individual.

At this stage, anyone who is considered high functioning and capable (or close to capable) of independent living should be referred to a rapid rehousing program. There will always be issues with the financial ability to maintain a household after the initial deposits and rents have been paid. The rapid rehousing case manager will have to assist clients in finding solutions to these. These case managers would also need links to other county services available to assist with issues that might arise. Case managers should be assigned for a minimum of 12 months, with a maximum of twenty clients. The goal is to check all the boxes that would be required to remain self-sufficient, including alcohol and drug recovery. We need to find the appropriate treatment plans that address these issues without persecution of the individual. What kind of safety net do we have for the individuals and families who can't maintain their housing on the first try?

Historically, we saw very credible success rates for homeless individuals who started their work at shelters that included alcohol and drug recovery programs. After just 90–120 days of clean time and 3–5 recovery meetings per week, there were significant results with improved stabilization. Having the opportunity to move on to another level of service for life skills training, vocational training, and some barrier reduction greatly elevates a person's chance to find meaningful work and take the first big step toward independence. This model requires reintroducing some form of transitional housing. With the right minds at work, there could be many alternatives to discuss on the types of housing, services, and community size needed to accommodate this form of programming.

Transportation will remain an obstacle, so location of these service models needs to be well planned. There are good reasons to consider alcohol and drug recovery options in shelters, along with triage services. During the time we have worked with the homeless, we have seen many cases where severe mental health characteristics were substantially abated after a few weeks of being clean, particularly when dealing with methamphetamines. This could be the difference between determining whether an individual is placed into permanent supportive housing or is eligible for further rehabilitation.

Our community, like most, needs to increase the number of mental health specialists who can do meaningful work with the homeless. It is critical to include alcohol and drug treatment for those with addiction, as an adjunct to a mental health strategy. Mental health specialists need to be available for clients in shelters, transitional housing programs, rapid rehousing programs, and permanent supportive housing programs. Having the proper diagnoses and medications for individuals can have a major impact on their ability to live independently.

Three other points of consideration for homeless services: The first is the ability to move laterally within a Continuum of Care for the specific purpose of allowing more people to finish programs that were started, regardless of setbacks, without major interruption of services. The current policy of listing someone as "not homeless" because they were "institutionalized" for 90 days creates roadblocks to recovery and should be reviewed. One of the obstacles to the system being proposed here is going to be the lack of organizations available to provide the services being recommended (at least in the early stages of rebuilding our system). It is why we need to prioritize the alignment of services to needs as soon as possible. The best long-term solution available includes moving large groups of our homeless people to independent living. If we can't do this, we may never have enough public services and housing solutions to meet the need. We have to look closely at where the money is being spent today in county and city budgets. There may be more there than we think or know.

The second point is the need to add physical health and sports therapy where possible. The body and the mind work together. When one is impaired, it has significant impact on the other. Sports can provide another important link to the community. We have proof that these activities have positive impact. They worked at Mather and are working today in the private sector, as we highlighted in Lisa Wrightsman's story. Lisa's work leading the women's homeless street soccer program is much more about rehabilitating lives than it is about playing soccer. And because she can point to so many successes, she has been able to raise corporate dollars to support her program.

That leads us to the third consideration. When we produce outcomes that show the leaders in our community we are improving the lives of the disenfranchised, we create even more support. This support comes to programs that move groups of people out of homelessness for good. Our history shows that putting people back to work and allowing them to leave homelessness behind creates the desire in our corporate community to want to play a part. We all get to share stories that make everyone proud of the work being done. Currently, those collective opportunities are disappearing instead of growing. There will always be a need for permanent supportive housing for some of our homeless. But many of our homeless want and deserve more. It is why there were always hundreds of people on the Mather waiting list. Moving people into storage containers, tent cities, or shelters that will never offer them the critical services needed to start the work to self-sufficiency feels like a job half done. We are better than that, and the growing population of homeless deserves better; and based on our experience, many want that chance.

Since the time I started writing this book, the University of California at Davis, through their Center for Healthcare Policy and Research, published a 130-page report titled *Integrating Care for People Experiencing Homelessness: A Focus on Sacramento County* (February 2020).[38] This report contains significant data and related information on the issues that were presented in this book. The issues that are raised and the conclusions that are presented in this report, in my opinion, validate virtually every point that has been made in this book, particularly the need for integrated services in homeless housing programs. The second sentence of this report states that during 2019 an estimated ten thousand people experienced homelessness in Sacramento County. This is far above any number that has been officially reported.

In a separate addendum to the report, *Economic Analysis of Options for Helping People Experiencing Homelessness in Sacramento*, the authors present a model of a single site integrated community

38 Melnikow, Ritley, Evans, et al. *Integrating Care for People Experiencing Homelessness: A Focus on Sacramento County* (Davis, CA: University of California, Davis: Center for Healthcare Policy and Research, February 2020).

design. It is complete with recommendations on size, number, and types of housing units, and recommendations on services. If you take the time to read it, you will find that with only a few minor exceptions, it mirrors the Mather Community Campus design. In the report, there is an estimated cost to build out this new community design. Without the twenty-five acres of land needed, the estimated costs range between a low of $194 million and a high of $255 million. On top of the cost to do this project, the property would have to be located and purchased, use permits would have to be secured, and an environmental impact study completed and approved. That would be followed by architecture being completed, building plans approved, permits obtained, and eventually the community would have to be constructed. Based on my background in the building industry, I think that with extreme good fortune this process would take at least 5 and possibly as long as 10 years. You would end up with a facility that had the same (albeit newer) facilities as Mather Community Campus. If this doesn't validate to anyone reading this document how seriously we are underutilizing that facility, I do not know what else to say. The cost to build this recommended campus would provide robust and complete services to more people than you could cram into that campus over the next 10 years. And it could be partially operational, with improvements, in under 18 months. I do agree that additional communities offering these integrated services should be planned, but we don't have to wait 5 to 7 years and we don't have to spend $200 million to $300 million to get started.

CHAPTER 13

Some Conclusions

IT IS UNCERTAIN HOW FAR ALONG WE ARE ON THE SCALE of social unrest, when it comes to the issues of the homeless; their impact on local commerce, the strain on public services, public nuisance complaints, public health issues, and the long-term financial burden of care going forward. The journey we are on has already cast aside a large contingent of quality service providers in an effort to provide more housing options. We are talking about people who had the rare combination of compassion, expertise, and experience to provide the effective services necessary to permanently move large groups of people out of homelessness for good.

Several reports have been published that include data on the success of rapid rehousing programs after 1 or 2 years. That is too short a period of time to make an accurate assessment of someone's (or some family's) ability to maintain a household once the rent subsidies have ended and the short-term case management has left (both of which usually last 3 to 6 months). The problems that developed over a lifetime will rarely disappear with 6 months of subsidy payments and light case management, especially when there are no requirements for the clients to accept other public services. We are still talking about the negative impacts of living on the street, including substance abuse and mental impairment. It is difficult to know which comes first: mental health or substance abuse. We do know these impairments are often the result of trauma caused by domestic violence, living on the streets, or early childhood abuse—the same issues prevalent in the client stories presented earlier.

It is impossible to tell how close we are to finding our community in a place where these issues are completely unmanageable. It is disconcerting that we seem to have a number of issues going in the wrong direction at the same time. We haven't discussed the fact that the supply of affordable housing options is disproportionate to the growing demand. At the same time, we are facing a decrease in our ability to pay for a growing need in public services. There are more influences at work that suggest we have already waited too long to demand change. The potential community impact, even dismissing the health-related issues, suggests a demand for public services that far outweighs the capacity to provide them.

It is time to look at ideas of how to move forward and make constructive change. That process needs to include the leaders in the community from the areas highlighted above. It is easy to be critical of the 10-year plans that have been developed in the past by individuals in local government. Those plans lacked vision, they were developed by government agencies that were limited in their access to the community assets needed to create a truly effective plan. We may not be able to directly control agencies like HUD, who refuse to fund the services needed to work on substance abuse, mental health, and barrier reduction. That doesn't mean we have to ignore those real problems in a new 10-year plan. These are the issues that the local community has to embrace as part of innovative solutions in a future plan to end homelessness. Even though it sounds daunting, everything about treating the issue of homelessness needs to be readdressed. It can no longer be that "thing" we need to address outside of our normal business plan. Instead, it merits a community action disaster plan with all hands on deck.

It is not practical to expect the local city or county government entities to develop plans and manage all of the issues of ending homelessness as it stands today. It is unfair to them and a disservice to the community to expect that system to produce the desired results. First, they are under far too much pressure to deliver results. Second, there are far too many elements to deal with that are out of their control. Third, there are far too many areas of expertise needed to create sound planning for what is now a very large population. Despite some earlier criticism of financial management on this issue, there may not be nearly enough money to take on all of the related elements that come with homelessness at the current level. We still need to do a critical financial evaluation of government budgeting to evaluate the scope of work that is expected. It is a way to possibly reduce waste, but the probability is that the government funds are short of what is needed to make a sizable impact on reducing homelessness.

Ending homelessness needs to be treated as a community opportunity project. In the same vein that community economic councils are created to collectively pursue economic growth and prosperity in a region, we need a "Community Council to End Homelessness" to develop the resources needed to fully dissect these issues and provide sound planning (including the financial plan) to address each one. We are led like sheep with the unchallenged policies of our government agencies. Public hearings do not seem to put enough pressure on public officials to cause significant change.

Besides, at the local level they lack the power and the resources to solve the problem.

Somehow, we need take on these issues with some dynamic, civic-minded collaboration that can force constructive change without violence and property damage. We always seem to wait too long to avoid the predictable consequences of our own inactions.

I know for a fact that getting this kind of change implemented is very difficult and frustrating. I traveled a few years ago to Washington, DC, with a large group of leaders in our community to have discussions on the homeless issues in Sacramento. That trip was part of an annual lobbying effort that is led by the Sacramento Chamber of Commerce. The year I went, homelessness was the number one issue on our agenda. We met with congressmen and women, senators, and leadership at HUD. In one meeting I attended with a member of the Congressional Committee on Appropriations, we asked about allocating additional federal funding for this issue. The congressman we met with just laughed and asked us where we expected it to come from, considering there was a balance budget amendment recently passed. Our team had a lot of meetings and heard a lot of concern from those we met with, and then nothing changed. Part of our solution has to include a different approach that can bypass years of lobbying to create change.

If we are to create significant change with the issue of our unsheltered population, we need to have representation from all leaders in our community. We have to start a discussion on where the current model of homeless care is leading and what changes have to happen to slow the growth. We need thought leaders from our higher education system, business community, health care, and the faith community, along with political leaders who are willing to take on the status quo in the current government system of setting funding priorities. Hopefully, we can influence the LONG-TERM planning in our community that might lead us in a more thoughtful and compassionate direction for homeless care, one that includes future outcomes we can all feel good about.

Epilogue

THE SAD TRUTH IS THAT IN THE AREA OF HOMELESS SER-
vices, we are moving backward instead of forward when viewed from
a humanitarian perspective. It is very difficult to see a civic movement in that direction happening anywhere for the homeless. Com-
pounding the problem is the awareness that the HUD policies of
funding only Housing First programs and the ill-conceived rollout
of coordinated entry has placed a communication wedge in what
was the existing systems of the local Continuums of Care; systems
that had been developed over many decades that included regular
discussion on how best to serve the local homeless population. The
local continuum here had no part in the discussion of how best to
implement coordinated entry. Just this year in Northern California,
there is a new push to discuss ways to improve that system. It seems
like too little, too late, now that so many programs that did not fit
the Housing First model have disappeared, along with many of the
professionals who could have participated in those conversations.
We will see if "better late than never" is a more appropriate adage.

Any system that promotes involved compassionate local conversation usually leads to improved conditions in a community. When we throw in the towel and turn over our oversight responsibilities to a state or federal government, at some point, the local interests will be subordinated to the policies of bureaucrats who have little insight or concern with how those issues impact local citizens. This happens when the local community or state is not capable of adequately providing solutions. What typically follows, over time, is that the federal government steps in and provides oversight (control). It happens in the form of new policies, regulations, and changes to the law that prevents local leaders from developing targeted solutions for their community. The almost complete swing in homeless services to the Housing First model is a prime example. It was the result of overreliance on the federal government to provide funding to solve local problems.

What Happens When the Community Gets Behind the Work

Let's end this work with examples of how locally driven, humanitarian homeless services that welcome local input and direct involvement can unite a community and consistently provide results that everyone is proud of. Below is a list of the organizations, businesses, service providers, and government agencies that volunteered their time, money, products, and services over 20 years to the Mather Community Campus programs. Yes, there was HUD funding underneath, but it was set up to leverage local funds and private contributions to support the work. That element somehow has been lost in our community. We believe it was fueled by the outcomes the whole community could support; moving people from homelessness to independent living. The list is amazing even though it only includes a handful of the actual examples. I hope it inspires some to think about the possibilities of creating this kind of community support going forward. At this time, there does not seem to be any community-backed initiative to help move many of our homeless to independent living. It is one way we truly have an opportunity to care for this population going forward. But here is a partial list of those who contributed to the Mather employment program while it was functioning.

Sacramento County: The county of Sacramento provided additional funding to Mather to offset student-housing costs through the Department of Human Assistance. They also provided an annual Community Services Block Grant that provided funding for vocational training, certain work tools, and work clothes. Operating under dynamic leadership, DHA employees ran the One-Stop employment center for 20 years and provided compassionate energetic support and employment opportunities for all the Mather residents for many years. There was a concerted effort on their part to have the employment of this population be a pillar for ending homelessness. Their involvement was terminated under the guise of new funding guidelines.

The City of Rancho Cordova: Rancho Cordova formed a Community Action Committee to provide local oversight and support for homeless services that were being provided at Mather Campus. The committee (also referred to as the CAC board) met with program managers and residents quarterly to assess the programming, performance, and civic influence the campus provided as a part of their community. The committee supported the local schools' continuing involvement in the educational opportunities of the children housed at Mather, which included school board representation on the committee. They also encouraged adult participation in community events that were happening in the city, including event work at the annual Mather Air Show. Over the years, Mather residents participated in city sports programs, parades, and special children's events hosted by Rancho Cordova. The CAC board was composed of civic leaders who cared about their community and the success of the Mather students. The involvement from these civic leaders was much more than writing a check. There was a legal technicality that removed their authority.

Major Contributing Companies and Organizations

Men's Warehouse: This company donated suits, shirts, ties, and other professional items to our campus for 20-plus years, allowing thousands of students to dress appropriately for interviews and jobs.

Sleep Train: Sleep train provided thousands of mattresses over the years, allowing every new student to have a new mattress to start their stay. This company is no longer in business.

Bayside Church: Bayside has sent dozens of volunteers out to the Mather Campus for painting projects, every few years, where they have spent full days painting buildings, doors, and activity rooms. Bayside continues to actively support a number of social service initiatives in the community.

Church of Jesus Christ of Latter-day Saints: Every November, this organization would bring enough turkeys for our kitchen to prepare a holiday meal for the singles and enough additional turkeys so that every family had one to serve at Thanksgiving.

Home Depot: Home Depot has supplied paint, cabinets, and hardware to the campus on numerous occasions to help make improvements.

Wells Fargo: In addition to making substantial financial donations to Mather Campus, Wells Fargo consistently encouraged managers to participate in employment readiness training on the campus by assisting with the practice of mock interviewing. Hundreds of students benefited from this activity.

Golden One/US Bank/Safe Credit Union: These financial institutions sent volunteers to Mather to teach "Ready to Rent" classes focusing on money management and household budgeting. Over the years, they worked with thousands of our students in teaching this curriculum.

Les Schwab: Every year, Les Schwab does a toy drive to benefit the children of families at Mather during the holidays. They created an annual event that all the families looked forward to after Thanksgiving.

VSP: One of the largest manufacturing companies for eyeglass lenses, VSP shared their hiring strategies with Mather staff, which allowed them to prepare more than one hundred Mather students for jobs at VSP over a 2-year period.

Bonnie Plumbing: Bonnie Plumbing assisted in pre-employment training, regularly staffed job fairs and hiring events at Mather, and hired dozens of students over the years.

Clayton Homes: Formerly Karston Homes, this manufactured housing company hired more than thirty students over a 7-year period, many of whom were later promoted to supervisory roles. This Berkshire-Hathaway company featured their relationship with Mather Campus and the employment successes in their monthly newsletter.

I could fill up several pages with the names of the employers who showed up at the Mather semiannual job fairs, met with students, and put people to work. More than two hundred businesses hired students directly out of the Mather program. These were businesses that also provided multiple employment opportunities to the students. They were asking, "How can we collectively create more opportunities for more people to leave homelessness permanently?" As this is being written, a little over 1 year later, there is nothing left for these businesses and their employees to support, and so they have all moved on.

Thousands of students left with work and continued to increase their contributions back into the community. Hundreds of individuals contributed hundreds of thousands of dollars and hundreds of hours of time to claim a small piece of the pride that came with seeing people move to self-sufficiency. And now, there are amazing alumni who might never have made it without this programming.

Virtually all of this community support and the opportunity that it created has now left the Mather Campus. It left when the employment program was shut down. It is not coming back, because there are no employment-related services, life skill classes, credit repair specialists, vocational training opportunities, job fairs, or employment initiatives to support. This may be a common story all across our country at this point for the homeless.

These questions remain:

- Do we believe creating a path to self-sufficiency for a segment of this population is important?

- Do we care enough to want to force change?

- Where do we start, and who is willing to get involved?

- Do we believe the growing population of homeless presents a potential community crisis?

I believe the most important question being asked above has to do with caring. If we don't care enough to get personally involved with trying to end or drastically reduce the number of people who are homeless, the problem will continue to grow.

Author's Biography

Sherman Haggerty has a master's degree in management from the Peter F. Drucker Graduate Management program at Claremont College. He worked for 35 years in homebuilding and land development for two large public companies that eventually merged. The company held the distinction of being the largest builder in America for a period of time during his tenure. He was a division president in Houston, Phoenix, Tucson, and Sacramento. From 2005 to 2008, he held the position of regional vice president of Sacramento operations and was responsible for all operations in the region. In 2006, the Sacramento region's operating revenues topped $1 billion. He retired in 2008. While working in Sacramento, he served on the board of directors for the North State Homebuilders Association, acting as the chair in 2000. He also worked with a handful of those board members to start a new nonprofit in 1999 called HomeAid. That organization was developed as part of the National Homebuilding Association initiative to help supply new beds for the transitionally homeless in their communities.

He was asked to join the Volunteers of America board in 2005, where he served until December 2013. In 2010, he was voted into the California Homebuilding Foundation's Hall of Fame, based in part on the community service work he had been a part of in Sacramento. In January 2014, he voluntarily stepped down from the VOA board to run the daily operations at Mather Community, with the goal of growing their employment program. In the 6 years, he was responsible for the program, they served well over one thousand clients. Between August 2015 and April 2019, he completed a 3-year program to become an ordained minister with Volunteers of America, focusing his work on trauma and moral injury.

Personal Statement

In 2014, I gave VOA a 2-year commitment to work at Mather. I was still there when our program was closed in December of 2019. For me, it *is* personal. I ended up staying for the 6 years because I fell in love with the program, the students, the staff, and everything that we did to change the lives of people we were serving. There were some difficult times along the way, and some heartbreaking individual failures, but the incredible number of successes and the gratitude of the alumni overshadowed them. I was fortunate to preside over our largest graduating class ceremony of well over one hundred students in June 2017. We actually had over two hundred students finish the program throughout that year, but getting everyone back to walk at graduation in June was sometimes a challenge.

I have spent the last 4 years studying trauma, moral injury, and moral resiliency. I attended seminars at Princeton University and the University of Southern California, and submitted a dissertation on moral injury as part of the ordination work. Prior to the work on trauma and moral injury, I completed a self-study on alcohol and drug addiction, including a number of seminars and published works. After all of this time, I feel I have very good insights into the struggles that are a part of being homeless; I am not in the least a romantic about the topic. Homelessness, alcohol and drug addiction, trauma, and mental health are all related and usually co-occurring issues, and each one is mean-spirited on its own. Collectively, they pose an extremely difficult set of circumstances that require structured care to begin to reverse the impacts. There are also a number of physical impairments that develop after long periods of time on the streets with substance abuse. Placing individuals with these co-occurring disorders into housing without intensive services only touches the surface of the deep-seated issues facing most chronically homeless people. As I conclude this work, I have not seen any proof that there are comprehensive plans in place to adequately address these issues. I sincerely hope and pray in the time I have left, that there is a reimagining in this country on what we can accomplish with caring, kindness, and community involvement for our citizens who have become homeless.

Acknowledgments

I am writing this just prior to publishing. This section is for those people who helped me immeasurably "stay the course," and helped me through my first adventure at writing a non-fiction book. It was a lot more work than I thought it would be to just to get to this point, and there are a few special people to thank for their patience, encouragement, and help along the way. So here they are:

My wife and children: My wife helped through the struggle of making the difficult decision of whether to take on this project from the beginning. Once we got over that hurdle, she jumped in and did a number of early edits on at least half a dozen manuscript versions. She is too private to allow me to put her name in print, but she is too important to let this opportunity to say thank you again go by. My four children continue to be an endless supply of support and encouragement.

Leo McFarland: Early on I gave Leo one of the first draft of the manuscript. It was long before a number of edits for corrections, clarifications, and content that improved it dramatically. He did not tell me to stop. The thank you is really for 40 plus years of service to the homeless and disenfranchised people in our community. Through his leadership, he demanded very high levels of care and kindness from his employees to all those who came to Volunteers of America looking for help.

Kent Lacin: Kent is a former VOA board member and current friend. Kent did everything imaginable to support our work at Mather and to promote the importance of the program in the community. He also read through an early version of my manuscript and his comments were right on point. It took me awhile to realize that he was right on a number of points, but I never doubted his commitment to help.

Judy McGary: Judy is also a former and current VOA board member and great friend. I summoned Judy late in the process to see if she would read the last version of the manuscript and give me her thoughts. In addition to fulfilling that request, Judy is also helping me currently pursue some early marketing channels.

Skye Loyd: Skye edited this book. Her patience and professionalism were put to the test with this novice novelist. Having completed the editing process with her has given me a whole new respect for the value of a top notch editor. She is a true professional.

Sam Bass: Sam has been my principal contact at Izzard Ink Publishing. Sorting through the publishing options was a tedious and stressful process that left me with many questions about expectations. As of today, we are nearing the finish line, but everything to this point has been above expectations. Izzard Ink got high marks from the Association of Independent Authors, and Sam gets high marks from me. He has been informative, thorough, and prompt, and so far his recommendations have hit the mark.

A special acknowledgment goes to the students and the student/employees that I wrote about in this book who lived the Mather experience and flourished. Jack, Lisa, Sam, Mike, Beverly, and Jenna: These are five people selected out of thousands more who have not only separated themselves from the homeless experience, but have gone on to help and encourage and directly assist hundreds more to do the same. Their willingness to sit with me for hours and patiently tell their stories became very special gifts.

Lastly, in addition to all of the other employees that I wrote about in this book, I want to recognize KC, our head chef at the Mather Kitchen. She was in charge of the kitchen/dining hall for the 7 years that I was the director. KC was tasked with teaching every client who came through Mather, how to work in a commercial kitchen and responsible for keeping track of every student's community service hours. She supervised and participated in the making of almost every meal for 180 singles, three times every day seven days a week. She also ran our culinary school and made sure every student that went through her training got a decent paying job in the restaurant business. No one worked harder with less recognition. And.... she made the best chocolate chip cookies on the planet.

Index

CPSIA information can be obtained
at www.ICGtesting.com
Printed in the USA
LVHW111751251021
701494LV00012B/256/J